Forgotten Churches

Forgotten Churches

Exploring England's Hidden Treasures

Luke Sherlock

Illustrations by Ioana Pioaru

FRANCES
LINCOLN

Contents

Introduction   6

1 **Into the Peaks**
  An Antiquarian Obsession Begins   10

2 **England in Genesis**
  Into the World of the Anglo-Saxons   20

3 **The Conquest of England**
  The Legacy of the Normans   36

4 **The Gothic in England**
  A National Architectural Style Emerges   50

5 **Squires and Parsons**
  Georgian England   74

6   **The Place of Whispering Memories**
Travels to England's Most Atmospheric Churches   88

7   **A Tumultuous Land**
The Ruptures of History Writ in Stone, Wood and Metal   112

8   **The Connoisseur**
Searching for Treasures Within English Churches   128

9   **Journeys of Contemplation**
Calm in a Chaotic World   154

The Final Word   170

Index of Churches   174
About the illustrator   176

Introduction

The Hidden Churches of England

L ong I have wandered to the hidden churches of England. Past field, marsh and woodland. Beyond suburban estates and rushing commuter roads, to the quiet places where all is still. To sit and think for a time, and better know the story of a nation remembered by these stones.

I can't say how many parish churches I've visited. I lost count long ago. From the granite coastline of Cornwall, up through the limestone backbone of England to the remotest moors of the north; amid the swirling metabolisms of our greatest cities, down isolated country tracks where the local farmer approaches to ask if you are lost. All these places I have known.

Yet I'm by no means unique in happily suffering this affliction. There are people who have dedicated significant portions of their lives to visiting every last church in the labyrinth of English parish life. With more than 12,500 churches listed by Historic England, not to mention the cathedrals, ruins and myriad other assorted oddities such as holy wells and wayside crosses, it is a near impossible task to know them all – though some have tried.

Each must undertake their own particular journey to these places. All will take away something different from this pilgrimage to the nation's past, for the churches of England are many things. They are a spiritual inheritance, designed to soothe and awe. They are records of social and economic histories. They are home to some of the finest art in the land. They are all these things and so much more.

This book has been written to document my own footsteps down the old church lanes. Some years ago, at the very beginning of my church explorations, I started an Instagram account to do this. Back then I could never have imagined all the wonder I would see or the meaning this obsession would add to my life. It is therefore unsurprising that, faced with the task of producing a book on this topic, I at first felt slightly overwhelmed. Yet the answer to what this work should cover came to me one sunny afternoon, as I turned over in my mind all the loose themes I could easily jot down and say, 'This is why I've visited these places.'

As such, the book might seem slightly unusual. If that is so, I am glad. The chapters are structured to reflect what I personally have appreciated in all my church visits and walks – as it is my habit to head out on foot, cross-country, in search of some peace and beauty. Some of these chapters therefore cover architecture, some dramatic events, and others attempt to capture a certain era or atmosphere. There is only a general framework and I let myself be free in my choices. Hurriedly I scratched down the plan for these chapters, recalling the moments of discovery that will continue to fuel my wanderings until the last of my days.

I could have written a thousand more versions of this book, or chosen any number of alternative churches to feature. Even now I sometimes ask myself why Youlgreave in Derbyshire didn't make the cut, or why the Beauchamp Chapel in Warwick missed out. However, I've settled down into feeling increasingly comfortable with this terror of possibilities. This isn't a guidebook; nor is it an expert technical text. It is a work of amateur enthusiasm and passion, a glimpse into the endless fascinations afforded to me by England's churches and the landscapes they sit within.

I must mention that in contrast to my amateur enthusiasm the book has been crafted into an item of beauty thanks to the professional hand of Ioana Pioaru. When I first saw her illustrations I so dearly hoped she would join me on this publication journey. Not only did she agree to do so, but with a dedication that was beyond the call of duty. Her artistic passion is etched into each of her works. I trust you will agree, the resulting illustrations are spectacular.

My greatest hopes for the book are twofold. Firstly, that it can be a handsome record of the places I have seen and hold dear. This seems a valid enterprise in itself. Secondly, that I can better share my passion with others who are like-minded, and inspire a greater appreciation for the collective cultural treasure these buildings represent. If they aren't valued, we could lose so much; this would be to diminish ourselves.

Finally, the title: Forgotten Churches. I wanted a title to draw attention to some of the wonders of our nation, languishing in their forgotten corners. Weatherbeaten and forlorn, it's rare I visit a country church and anyone else is about. Even some of the London churches I cover in this book are relatively unknown. Take St Bartholomew-the-Great in Smithfield, one of the capital's finest medieval spaces. Thousands must walk past each day not knowing it exists. The visitor figures should be vastly higher than I know them to be. Of course, if you've purchased this book or been gifted it, it's unlikely such places are quite so forgotten by you. Even so, I never cease to be amazed by the parish treasures that sleep quietly behind stackable chairs and piles of hymn books. As such, I hope this work can contribute to a rising enthusiasm for these special churches and place them firmly at the heart of our thinking when it comes to conserving our heritage.

I have also chosen the word 'hidden' in the subtitle: 'Exploring England's Hidden Treasures.' Some of these churches might not strike the viewer as inconspicuous. For example, the dazzlingly grand church at Burford in the Cotswolds. However, while I have attempted to feature many churches that might be a little off the beaten track, I have also sought to reveal elements of their history that might be hidden away awaiting discovery. Therefore, I hope the reader will indulge this broad approach. In some ways, these churches are museums, but I wished to avoid this word choice in the title as they are also living, breathing community entities in many cases.

So, let us remember on those days when life might seem heavy and full of challenges, that the churches of England will be there waiting for us, as they have for generations. In their hushed cool interiors we can traverse the ping pong tables and Sunday School paraphernalia as the church guidebook quivers in our hands and we look through the gloom at the exalted monument to the sometime Lord So-and-so. Or if this isn't possible for you, due to distance or otherwise, this book and others can be on hand to enable you to escape through their pages to another place for a time. My eldest brother once gave me a landscape painting of his. On the back he'd written, 'Remember, you can always get away.' It's in this spirit that I offer this book to you.

Let us venture into the churches.

Into the Peaks

An Antiquarian Obsession Begins

Having applied for the job on a whim, one lunchtime, it
was much to my surprise that I learnt I would be the first
sustainability manager for the Devonshire Group, representing
the businesses and charitable interests of the Duke of
Devonshire. The summer of 2013 saw me packing up the house
I'd shared with a group of university friends, in London, to
relocate to the fairytale village of Edensor on the Chatsworth
Estate in Derbyshire. Although I'd grown up in the county, it
still felt slightly surreal to be moving into a cottage in one of the
most iconic and picturesque corners of the Peak District. Where
once there'd been the pubs and galleries of the capital, I would
now spend my weekends walking neighbours' dogs, preparing
for village socials, exploring remote footpaths and popping my
head into those quiet churches that dotted the landscape. An
antiquarian obsession was about to begin.

St Peter, Edensor Derbyshire

Edensor is a strange place. It's pronounced *'Enza'*. Between 1839 and 1843, the 6th Duke of Devonshire demolished the original village and moved it to its current position. There's a wall all the way around it. The story goes that this was so he'd have a better view from his windows up at the big house. Though widely accepted, it seems this version of events is slightly more complicated in reality. While certainly some aesthetic preoccupations also motivated the rebuild, the Duke was keen to improve living conditions for residents. I was once shown an old book thought to contain the European architectural styles the Duke had picked for his new village's unique, somewhat eccentric appearance: a gatehouse with embattled parapet, an Italian villa, a Swiss cottage, a Tudor lodge, and so on. I lived in 'Sunnybank', a more conventional chocolate box cottage. Yet somehow this motley assemblage of houses seems to work, all pinned to their little fold in the landscape by the soaring church spire of St Peter's.

That spire rises 166 ft. It's almost absurdly big. Yet amid the grandeur of this rolling 'Capability' Brown-designed landscape, it feels constrained and subdued. Architect Sir Gilbert Scott rebuilt the old Norman church in the 1860s. I had little interest in the church at first, though eventually the regular clang of the church bells called me into the churchyard to find the grave of Kathleen

'Kick' Kennedy (1920–1948), sister of JFK, who died in a plane crash, aged 28, in 1948.

Kathleen was married to William Cavendish, Marquess of Hartington (1917–1944), elder son of the 10th Duke of Devonshire. He died four years before Kathleen, shot just months after their wedding, while fighting for the liberation of Europe. A little Stars-and-Stripes flag fluttered at the foot of Kathleen's grave when I first stood before it. Her brother made a detour to Edensor while president, in June 1963. This is remembered by a little carved stone.

Inside the church, I found a glorious monument funded by the Marquess' ancestor, William Cavendish, 2nd Earl of Devonshire (1590–1628) to his father, William Cavendish, 1st Earl of Devonshire (1552–1626), and his uncle, Henry Cavendish (1550–1616). Both were sons of Bess of Hardwick and Sir William Cavendish. Henry, ten years dead when William died, appears as a skeleton on a straw mattress. In front of him is William, with a gaunt face in a shroud. To the left, stands Mars, god of war, to the right is Minerva, goddess of wisdom. The piece is crowned by the Cavendish arms, superbly carved and gilded.

St John the Baptist, Chelmorton Derbyshire

One summer's day, I decided to visit Chelmorton for the lack of anything else to do. I remembered visiting the village with my parents as a teenager. They are Derbyshire folk and, growing up in the county, I would often be dragged out to see some point of interest in the Peak District. My mum had been particularly enthusiastic about the patchwork of strip fields spreading their long fingers out from the centre of Chelmorton. I have no doubt I was thrilled to see these too, sulking behind my parents. And yet, they stuck with me, as these things tend to do.

This is wild upland Derbyshire, with few trees and pockmarked by a history of mineral extraction. With remnants of its medieval field system intact, rising up from the single street around which this linear settlement is clustered, there is something almost primitive about Chelmorton. To get a better view I ambled up Chelmorton Low, a round flat hill, up past the pub and the church. Gazing down, as the heat of the day licked me and insects buzzed around, I could see the footprint of the village. Lifting my head, I met the octagonal stone church spire at eye level. This is said to be the highest above sea level in England, at 1,209 ft. A golden locust glints from the weathervane above, the symbol of St John the Baptist himself. The spire was a fifteenth-century addition, whereas much of what stands below it was built in the thirteenth and fourteenth centuries. The church was locked though. I sat and had a refreshing pint outside the Church Inn. I would have to return another time.

St Mary & St Barlok, Norbury Derbyshire

I drove out to Norbury with my dad. We were repeating a journey he'd taken with my granddad back in the 1960s. This was 'the family church' where the Sherlock name and its variations appeared on the parish records, going back to at least the eighteenth century. Quite how long the Sherlocks had been in this part of the world seems to be obscured by the mists of history. Yet in my family lore, this is where we are from.

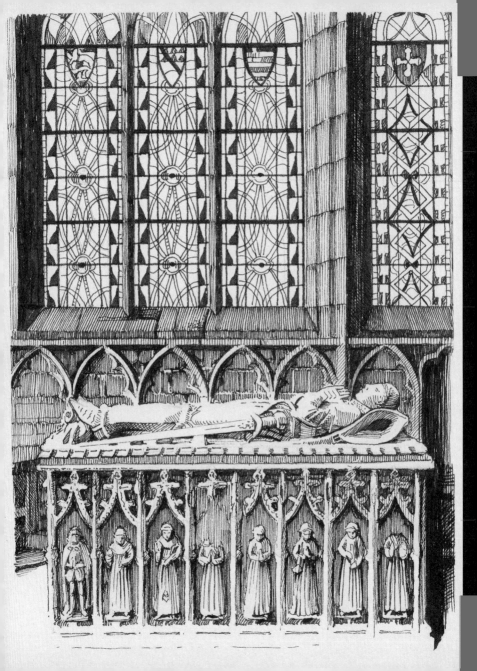

Today, Norbury is an out of the way place on the banks of the River Dove. St Mary's and St Barlok's stands at the back of an expansive churchyard beside Norbury Hall, now owned and let out by the National Trust. There is little else here. Construction of the church began in 1295, the chancel built first, followed over the next 200 years or so by nave and transepts. It is the chancel that ranks among the first-class wonders of English architectural history.

Upon entering, a gloomy nave leads you into an astonishing lantern of light. The glass was inserted in the first years of the fourteenth century and still filters warm rays into a sanctuary of calm. No doubt this is some of the finest early medieval glass in the country. It was made to link the Fitzherbert family, who had held the manor of Norbury since 1125, to royalty and the leading noble families of the land. In total no fewer than 25 shields of arms are displayed in this glorious panoply of high medieval society.

Beneath the filtered light sit the Fitzherbert monuments in milky Chellaston alabaster. On the right is Nicholas Fitzherbert (c.1410–73). Here Nicholas wears a collar decorated by suns and roses, referencing the white rose of York. The sun emblem of King Edward IV (1442–1983; r.1461–70, 1471–83) – taken from the Battle of Mortimer's Cross when combat was preceded by a meteorological phenomenon known as a parhelion, which consists of bright spots either side of the sun, a portent to his

eventual victory. For me, it is a thing of near unfathomable beauty and wonder that this object, capturing so perfectly the high Gothic romance and drama of the Wars of the Roses, sits quietly in the Peak District countryside. Across from Nicholas sits a tomb chest to his son, Ralph Fitzherbert (d.1483), 12th Lord of the Manor, and his wife, Elizabeth Marshall (d.1490). Beneath the effigies, their children mourn, carved as 'weepers' into the side of the tomb. Near Ralph's feet a little bedesman thumbs his rosary.

These monuments represent some of the finest examples of medieval craftsmanship. My ancestors would have sat among those pews, staring forward at the same view as I had. How strange it was to know this, to be in that same space. I now return to this church every couple of years or so. A pilgrimage of sorts. I'm yet to encounter another soul.

St John the Baptist, Tideswell Derbyshire

I approached the church with some trepidation. I wasn't sure if it would be open in the evening, even though it was summer and still light. Somehow, I felt a little out of place. I was visiting the 'Cathedral of the Peaks', so named for its considerable size: it dominates the centre of the village. This was the first time I'd ever travelled specifically to see a church and just as I was about to try the big wooden door, it swung open.

'Here for the talk?' enquired the vicar ushering me inside. *The talk?* This was a mistake. Sensing my panic and confusion, he continued, 'There's a local photographer giving a presentation in a few minutes. On the history of the church. His lens has got right up in the rafters!' I shuffled forward and slid into one of the pews at the back.

Construction of St John's took place between 1320 and 1400, straddling the devastations caused by the Black Death, when all building work halted for several decades. The tower and chancel were added in the late-fourteenth century with elements of a new architectural style: the 'Perpendicular Gothic'. The photographer pointed out elements of this new style, and, although I was utterly baffled, I was, nonetheless, fascinated by the idea of being able to date these special buildings from such stylistic observations.

Soon we moved from the pews and were huddled together in the vast chancel peering below the tomb to Sir Samson Meverill (1388–1462) who once fought in France against Joan of Arc (c.1412–31). He is depicted in the form of a stone cadaver, a type of *memento mori* popular in the late Middle Ages. Dusty, cobwebbed and out of view, it was eerie and somehow thrilling to hunch down and spy Sir Sampson's emaciated figure, cradled by angels. I'd have never thought to look here if it wasn't for the guide that day. What else had I been missing?

Elsewhere, I learnt of local stonemasons and woodcarvers, a mysterious fourteenth-century alabaster tomb known as the 'de Bower' monument, featuring the effigies of Sir Thurstan and Lady Margaret de Bower, 'hatchments', glass, screens and more. After saying my thanks for all this knowledge, I walked back to my car in the cooler dusk, knowing I'd be visiting many more of these buildings.

England in Genesis

Into the World of the Anglo-Saxons

Once there was an England before England. A land of rival
kingdoms, the fortunes of which rose and fell across the
centuries following the withdrawal of the Roman Legions. A
place where Vikings raided and plundered and settled, pushing
westward until the defiance of Wessex and the eventual
consolidation of the English Crown under Æthelstan in 927.
During these long centuries of shifting political and cultural
primacy, the seed of Christianity was planted in English soil;
a seed that would germinate into a deeply Christian society.
Of course, Christianity had been here before, kindled in the
scattered windblown ruins of the former Roman settlements
the Anglo-Saxons would find abandoned and decayed. It had
never, in fact, left. On the margins of the island, native Britons
kept the worship of Christ alive, and an Age of Saints can still
be recalled in obscure church dedications. The story of how
Christianity came to be consolidated into the religion of the
English has long captivated me. I have come to realise that the
stones of England still memorialises these times, a flickering
material connection to the flame of our past.

All Saints, Brixworth Northamptonshire

As Christianity spread throughout England, stone wayside crosses were erected, as well as churches of wood and, increasingly, as the centuries rolled on, of stone. Of those wooden churches, there are but a few tantalising remains. Yet some of the most important stone Anglo-Saxon buildings still stand. In fact, hundreds of pre-Conquest architectural features are to be found in the churches of England. Some are near complete Anglo-Saxon structures; others harbour only fragmentary glimpses of what would have once been.

One of the first Anglo-Saxon churches, I saw with my own eyes was Brixworth. Highlighting the importance of this building, the architectural historian Sir Alfred Clapham (1883–1950) once described it as 'perhaps the most imposing architectural memorial of the seventh century yet surviving north of the Alps'. To be in the presence of such buildings is to physically embrace the origin story of our island life.

The central nave and arcades are thought to survive from the late seventh century, when Mercian kings and queens controlled the area. The west tower was likely extended in the tenth century, with the spire arriving much later in the fourteenth century. At the time of the original construction, bricks and tiles were reused from a nearby Roman settlement. It was a building undertaken on a monumental scale, a basilica some 160 ft in length and characteristically high, as was the Anglo-Saxon inclination for interior volume. A semicircular 'apse' would have once sat at the east end – a feature rather crudely reconstructed by the Victorians – as well as five 'porticus' rooms lining each side of the church.

A building on this scale puts Brixworth not only among the finest of surviving Anglo-Saxon churches in England but at the vanguard of European architectural achievements at this time. In many ways, it anticipates the burst of architectural energy and creativity later seen in the Carolingian Empire and under Charlamagne (c.748–814; variously reigned as King of the Franks, Lombards and Emperor, 768–814) who succeeded in uniting Western and Central Europe under the banner of Rome.

St Martin, Canterbury Kent

On a cold overcast day, I walked through the inner suburbs of Canterbury to the oldest church in continuous use in the English-speaking world. It dates back to the second half of the sixth century and once acted as the private chapel of Queen Bertha of Kent (c.565–c.601). As a Christian–Frankish princess, Bertha was permitted by her pagan husband, Æthelberht, King of Kent (r.560–616), to continue practising this alien religion under the guidance of a personal chaplain brought over from the continent, Bishop Liudhard. Some have even speculated the church could have been in continuous use since the Roman occupation, though it seems likely Æthelberht restored the building for his queen, whatever its original purpose. Long thin Roman bricks can still be seen on the sides of the chancel. The east end of the church dates from the twelfth and thirteenth centuries and the prominent tower was added in the fourteenth century.

When Augustine and his entourage arrived from Rome on their famous papal mission to convert the Anglo-Saxons in 597, this chapel became their base. As St Bede (c.672/3–c.735) was to write, 'here they first began to assemble, to sing the psalms, to pray, to celebrate mass, to preach and to baptise, until the king was converted to the faith and gave them greater freedom to preach and to build and restore churches everywhere'. It

is, therefore, little surprise that along with Canterbury Cathedral and St Augustine's Abbey, St Martin's forms part of the Canterbury World Heritage Site. Sadly, it doesn't feel that way. This astonishing building, a near uninterrupted thread to the establishment of the Christian faith on this land, and all this has meant, sits forlorn, often locked, away from the buzz of the mass of tourists visiting the city less than half a mile away.

I noticed the *Via Francigena* passes through the churchyard, as marked by some signs on the ground. I'd read about this ancient pilgrimage route from Canterbury to Rome, some 3,000 km, in Guy Staggs' remarkable book, *The Crossway*, though he went on to finish in Jerusalem. The opening steps were enough for me as I headed down to the nearby village of Patrixbourne to see an old Norman door before turning tail and getting the train back to London.

St Peter-on-the-Wall, Bradwell-on-Sea Essex

You have to walk a little way down to the Chapel of St Peter-on-the-Wall, where flat fields give way to a huge wind buffeted sky on the southern bank of the Blackwater Estuary. The chapel was constructed after St Cedd (c.620–c.664) arrived in the 650s to found a missionary and monastic Christian community in the Kingdom of the East Saxons. It's among the oldest of Christian buildings in England.

Cedd had been a follower of Aidan of Lindisfarne (d.651) and following successful missions to the Mercian Kingdom in the Midlands, it is likely he sailed to shore near a former Roman military station at the invitation of a king, likely Sigeberht the Good (d. c.653–664). We can imagine Cedd instructing the construction of a small temporary wooden structure – the project to build a larger stone sanctuary was realised over time. As we have seen elsewhere, St Peter's was built by recycling Roman materials close to hand. An original apse can still be traced on the ground. With walls well over 20 ft, how thrilling it must have been for the leaders of these kingdoms to propagate the new beliefs in such a way. The ever-lyrical chronicler of the English counties Arthur Mee (1875–1943) commented of Bradwell-on-Sea, that it is 'one of the forgotten wonders of our motherland, with a story and spectacle that must stir our hearts. We are here at the dawn of our history.'

It isn't anything like the churches we commonly imagine. The interior of the church is bare. A few benches line the walls but there are no pews. A modern stone altar and cross installed after the Second World War are the only other decoration, save for a few candleholders. Most of the light comes from the open door. It's a simple space – but no less for it.

Beyond its remarkable history, this is a landscape to be cherished. There is something otherworldly about the waves lapping against the thick mud of the Dengie Peninsula marshes, the hedgerows alive with the sounds of wildlife. In a grove of trees behind this natural 'wall' that separates it from the North Sea, lies the Christian community of Othona, so named after the Roman fort that was once on this site. Othona is concerned with living in harmony, both with nature and with each other. It was born as a place for reflection and reconciliation after the chaos of the Second World War. I can only imagine what it was like to be out here, by the campfire on a starry night, yards from the crash of the sea, after the ravages and trauma of war.

The now decommissioned Bradwell nuclear power station can be seen, reminding us that this isn't bucolic England. It is raw and exposed, perhaps even vulnerable. Yet the old chapel still stands. I love returning to this special place.

St Lawrence, Eyam Derbyshire

Eyam is famous for a tragic reason. This is where a flea-infested parcel of cloth brought the plague from London in late August 1665. As disease and death spread, the newly appointed rector, William Mompesson (1639–1709), decided to act. He needed help, though, as he had only arrived in Eyam in April 1664, replacing Thomas Stanley (1610–70). Stanley had refused the 1662 Act of Uniformity and the Book of Common Prayer. In this Puritan-leaning area, Mompesson was treated with suspicion. The two men were to agree on an astonishing plan. There would be a quarantine. Nobody would leave the village. Nobody would arrive. Church services would be held in the open air. The dead would be buried quickly near where they fell. Today, footpaths will lead you to boundary stones where holes were drilled so money could be left in vinegar as payment for goods. It's a ghostly experience to walk to one such stone on the way to the neighbouring village of Stoney Middleton.

These courageous and heartbreaking actions likely saved much of northern England from similarly harrowing tragedies. Indeed, Mompesson's own wife, Catherine, died at the age of just 27 in August 1666. Her tomb can be found in the churchyard. The historic cottages of the village still have signs outlining the awful losses. In total, around 260 of 800 residents perished before the disease passed towards the end of 1666.

Yet there is much of note in Eyam beyond the drama of the seventeenth century. As Christianity established itself in Anglo-Saxon England, stone crosses became an important feature of the spiritual landscape. The example at Eyam is one of the best-preserved Mercian crosses in the Midlands and is thought to date from the eighth or ninth century. Found on a moor in the eighteenth century, and subsequently moved to the south side of the churchyard, it would have originally been erected to gather the faithful for Christian instruction. Beautifully sculpted, and eight foot high, it displays angels, the Virgin and Child, and elaborate scroll-work carvings, still visible to this day.

The late twelfth- and early thirteenth-century core of the church is largely as it would have been at the time of the plague, but a Victorian rebuilding project has significantly changed the aisles, chancel and porch. Nevertheless, the spirit of Mompesson lives on. His chair and pulpit take prime position. Perhaps it was from this very pulpit that he informed the congregation of the plan to deal with the plague. It is also worth noting the sixteenth- and seventeenth-century wall paintings on the nave walls. The stained glass mostly comes from the Victorian restorations, but a 'plague window', relaying the story of those dreadful years, was installed in 1985.

St Mary, Breamore Hampshire

I travelled out to Breamore on my only day off work in a six-week stretch. At the time, I was setting up a new independent bookshop and my head was full of tasks to complete. I sensed I needed a break from it all, at least for a moment. And what better way to pause than take in some mighty Saxon architecture? On arrival at Breamore, the long-and-short work of the porticus jumped out at me, where the corner 'quoin' stones are quite literally long and then flat (short), long and then flat, and so on. There are few clearer signs of great age than a bit of solid long-and-short work.

St Mary's is thought to have been financed by Æthelred II the Unready (c.966–1016; r. 978–1016). It would have been a minster on a royal estate and, despite some quintessential Anglo-Saxon features, is quite unlike other churches I have seen from this period. Here, the emphasis seems to be on the tower, which remains original. This is vast when compared to the south porticus room attached to it and which would have once been matched by a fellow porticus on the north side, where the roofline is still visible. With these additions, the church shows some movement towards the cruciform plan that would become common in later English churches.

The church has seen many alterations and additions. The fourteenth century saw perhaps the most noticeable changes with the chancel rebuilt. The early sixteenth-century chapel, raised above the twelfth-century porch beneath, is particularly enjoyable. It was designed to protect a precious carved relief, Saxon 'rood' (taken from the Anglo-Saxon for cross) from the elements, after it had been moved to face all those entering the church in the fifteenth century. This sculptural work can still be seen today.

For all the architectural fireworks of the exterior, it's the interior that harbours St Mary's greatest treasure: a tantalising glimpse of the Anglo-Saxon tongue. *HER SWUTELATH SEO GECWYDRAEDNES THE* is inscribed above the south porticus arch. Roughly this translates as, 'here is manifested the word to thee.'

As I left, I noticed what seemed to be a Puritan warning on the outer wall of the church. Perhaps it was added in the seventeenth century. The message was a simple one: *'avoyd fornication'*.

St Laurence, Bradford-on-Avon Wiltshire

Early Christian missionaries would have set up altars besides preaching crosses, open to the howling winds and lashing rains. Protection from the elements was necessary in order for the ceremony of the mass to be observed in relative comfort. And so England's early churches came to be. Here at St Laurence, we can see that reality in the thick ashlar stone raised around 1000. To sit on the nave benches and look into the chancel of this little chapel is to contemplate Anglo-Saxon worship at the dawn of England itself.

This is a simple and powerful building. A two-cell structure of central nave and chancel with rear porticus. The chancel is a small cocoon, cave-like, the holy centre of the mass ceremony – a dim, mysterious space where shafts of light illuminate the altar from a rudimentary Anglo-Saxon window. The reconstructed altar incorporates carved stonework likely even older than the present church. Above this a sculptural triptych has been put in place, featuring a decorative Anglo-Saxon block, a fragment of fossilised tree, and a twisting stone ring, sculpted by the artist John Maine in 2012. I find this ensemble subtle and sympathetic. Others may disagree.

Back in the nave are two angels high up either side of the narrow chancel arch. These are Anglo-Saxon angels and the keystones to the remarkable rediscovery of this building. For centuries the true history of St Laurence's was lost. The building had been used variously as a charnel house, a school and even as a cottage. It was in the 1850s when historian Canon Jones (1817–85) of the nearby Holy Trinity Church noticed its roofline amid the ramble of surrounding buildings and thought something about it looked intriguing, that the true origins of the building were revealed. Taking a closer look, he spied the remarkable carved angels high up on the walls. In the following decades, a trust was founded to acquire and oversee the church's restoration.

I feel an intense calm pressing in from those big old stones at St Laurence's. On my last visit, I shared a familiar nod of recognition with a dog walker who was settling down for a moment of rest. Here we find England in genesis, ritual expression in heavy stone. A rugged structure to shelter a strengthening faith.

St John the Baptist, Barnack Cambridgeshire

The two stage Anglo-Saxon tower at Barnack dates from around 1000–20. Its early Gothic spire is a relative newcomer, having been added around 1200. We can accept a bit of sympathetic modernism such as this in our church buildings. Built in two powerful square stages, held in place by heavy corner quoins, each side of the tower holds original decorative sculptural work – a cockerel and other beasts are visible for those strong of eye, alongside a splendidly simple triangular window up top. With vertical pilaster stripwork, there is something aesthetically pleasing about Barnack, more so than I've often found to be the case in Anglo-Saxon buildings. This said, the tower is all that remains of the original structure.

Inside we can see the strength and ambition of a church building from this period. The tower arch here is 13 ft wide, 20 ft high, and no nonsense. The only other item within the church that may be pre-Conquest is a magnificent Christ in the act of benediction, found buried under the north aisle in 1931. This sculpture has divided opinion as to its age, with the carving thought to date anywhere between the eleventh and thirteenth centuries depending on which expert you ask. The architectural historian Alec Clifton-Taylor (1907–85) seemed particularly enthused by his viewing of this work, describing it as, 'the essence of

nobility and dignity'. Whatever the reason, to be able to see that raised hand in blessing, flecks of original colouring still visible, no matter how old is a privilege.

The church is built from coarse creamy brown-coloured, Barnack-oolitic limestone, of which many churches in this wider region were constructed, as well as several cathedrals. The original quarry, just to the south of the village, was once one of the most important in medieval England. What life and vibrance these little streets must have seen.

As I left the church, I returned to the doorway in the south face of the tower. This may be the most iconic Anglo-Saxon architectural feature I've ever seen. It shouts out its great age. It is simple. It is crude. It has endured a thousand winters.

The Conquest of England

The Legacy of the Normans

There is considerable academic debate about the impact of the
Norman Conquest on church architecture in England. The
term 'Romanesque' is often used to describe churches built
in the century or so following 1066, or more simply 'Norman.'
Romanesque is a reference to the architecture of early Christian
Rome. For simplicity's sake, I have often used these terms
myself. Some find them too crude and prefer 'Anglo-Norman',
emphasising the unique burst of architectural creativity at
this time, drawing on local skills, techniques and aesthetic
programmes but bolstered by fresh imperial ambition and the
continental influences that had been seeping into the land for
centuries. Whatever the case, the Conquest gave unprecedented
impetus to the construction and reconstruction of late English
churches. The church was reorganised, wealth flowing in from
penitent Norman landholders, and masons were given the
opportunity to cut and carve some of the most startling,
playful, powerful and culturally eclectic architecture ever
seen on these shores.

St John's Chapel, Tower of London Greater London

The Chapel of St John was commissioned by William the Conqueror (*c.*1028–87; r.1066–87) as the spiritual heart of his glistening, domineering White Tower, within the wider fortress-like Tower of London complex in London. Framed by powerful columns, elaborated by precise stone carving on the capitals, large enough to accommodate a gallery and religious processions along the aisles – this was ecclesiastical architecture to make a statement. However, William wouldn't live to supplicate his God from within this spectacular expression of royal piety. He died in 1087 before its completion, and it would be left to subsequent kings and queens to worship here beside their chaplains and households.

Entering this private core of the new imperium is to be in awe. I'd long avoided the Tower while living in London. Rightfully, it is deluged by tourists and far away from the quiet corners of the land I usually seek out.

After the COVID-19 restrictions were lifted, and tourist attractions began to cautiously reopen, I spotted my opportunity. The usual gushing stream of tourist traffic was but a trickle. For a full half-hour, I basked in the glory of the chapel in near solitude. Every now and then someone wandered by and lingered for a moment before heading onto the other glories of the Tower, but this is what I was here for: to inhale the drama and history these stones had witnessed.

During the Peasants' Revolt of 1381, a mob burst into the chapel and seized the Archbishop of London, Simon Sudbury, as he prayed at the altar. He was dragged away and executed. His leathered head, scorched on the pike-end of a rowdy English summer, eventually made its way back to his hometown of Sudbury, Suffolk, where it is still housed in the Church of St Gregory. I have been there and it has a fine font cover, too.

St Mary & St David, Kilpeck Herefordshire

All my life I will remember walking up to the wild and mysterious church at Kilpeck. A riot of Norman carvings greeted me at the south doorway – a writhing phantasmagoria of the twelfth-century imagination. Moving into the churchyard, the morning silhouette of the Black Mountains beyond amplified the sensory drama.

Following William the Conqueror's invasion of England, Kilpeck was given to his kinsman William fitz Norman (c.1048–c.1071). William's son, Hugh, sometime Keeper of the King's Forests, instructed the creation of this remarkable building before it was gifted to Gloucester Cathedral in 1134. From documentary evidence, we know there was a church building here from at least 650. As with so many of those given lands in the wake of the Conquest, Hugh would have been elevating the worship of their providential lord.

Cut from pinkish sandstone, the church has survived these near 900 years in remarkably good condition. It represents a time when a whole host of cosmopolitan architectural and stylistic traditions were influencing the buildings of England. Indeed, Kilpeck is perhaps the most famous example from the Herefordshire School of stone carvers – a collective term for the distinctive and playful output of twelfth-century masons operating in this area, who would have taken inspiration from a range of diverse sculptural traditions, French, Germanic, Scandinavian, Anglo-Saxon and a wider circle of cultural exchange.

Moving away from the masterful south doorway, the visitor's attention is drawn to no less than 85 corbel carvings. Some of these are thought to be symbols taken from medieval bestiaries – compendiums of beasts to provide moral instruction from all of God's creation. Other figures defy clear explanation and appear to document everyday life:

tumbling wrestlers, musicians, and even a juggler.

One of the most commented upon corbels is a sheela-na-gig, an architectural grotesque not so uncommon to Romanesque churches. While this figure shows a woman holding open her vulva, prudish Victorian society recast it as a woman baring her heart to God.

The Kilpeck church guidebook wonderfully describes some of the speculation around these sheela-na-gigs as 'a device to ward off evil spirits, a fertility cult figure, a representation of the Great Earth Mother Goddess, a Celtic goddess of creation and destruction, an obscene hag, a sexual stimulant, a medieval *Schandbild* to castigate the sins of the flesh.' There are thought to be over 30 such carvings that survive in England. I will leave the true interpretation of Sheela-na-gigs to the ever-evolving interpretations of the academic experts.

Inside the magic continues.

Charming chancel arch figures are stacked one above the other. It has been speculated they were inspired by similar works on the Gate of the Silversmiths at the Cathedral of Santiago de Compostela. Stepping forward, you can see the apse contains a fine early example of rib vaulting, deeply cut with chevrons. Four heads look down on the altar. The sacred intensity of this small sheltered space remains unchanged since the days when Norman land holders would have knelt here in prayer, thankful for the grace and blessings of their Lord.

Hospital of St Cross and Almshouse of Noble Poverty, Winchester Hampshire

Cattle slumber in the water meadows of the River Itchen beside St Cross, a near cathedral scale almshouse of noble poverty. It was founded in around 1136 by Henry de Blois (c.1096–1171), Bishop of Winchester, half-brother of King Stephen (c.1092/96–1154; r.1135–54), during a time of great hardship, as England descended into a war of succession. The intention was to provide accommodation and food for 13 poor men, too frail to work, and feed 100 locals a day. As the 13 men were 'brothers' rather than monks, St Cross remained a secular foundation and, as such, escaped the full ravages of the dissolution of the monasteries. The hospital now houses 25 brothers in buildings that date from 1446. These brothers are either 'red' or 'black', according to their robes and concomitant membership of one of two medieval charitable foundations. For 800 years or more visiting pilgrims have requested the 'Wayfarer's Dole' from the Porter's Lodge, which can still be done. You get a horn of beer and a morsel of bread. It is nice that such civil oddities still exist in our world.

The church itself survives as an example of what has been termed late Norman architecture. By this, we can take it to capture the fullest confidence and grandeur ecclesiastical building work was to realise in the century following the Conquest. The walls are perhaps three-feet or so thick, packed with stone from as far away as Caen, on the northwest coast of France. Much of the east end of the church up to the central bays of the nave were constructed in the later-half of the twelfth century.

This imposing Norman work rises majestically over the riverside footpath when approached from the cathedral city less than a mile or so away. Round headed windows and an abundant, almost obsessive, predilection for crisp chevron ornamentation are indicative of the building's age. Pointed arches and the work of the west end of the nave, showcase an evolution in architectural practices, a transition deeper into the Gothic. However, to sit on the banks of the Itchen and doze under The Hospital of St Cross is to view one of the few continuous threads linking us to a lost age of medieval institutions largely smashed by the Reformation.

St Germans Priory, St Germans Cornwall

Norman doorways are a favourite of mine. Justifiably, locals are always proud of them. As the years have gone by and my posts on social media have gained some small degree of recognition and interest, followers have not infrequently told me of this spectacular Norman doorway and that, which they knew about and which I had to see. Dutifully, these kind recommendations have been noted and mentally stored for some future trip. Even so, somewhere in my mind I have always known that the visual festivities of St Germans' iconic west front would be near impossible to surpass. It is the greatest Norman doorway I've seen in any parish church in England.

Twenty-feet wide. Seven orders of zigzagging arches fan out, battered by the sea spit and salt winds of Cornwall. There might not be the curious carved decoration of other Norman works here at St Germans but what there is, in abundance, is thrusting architectural power. Above the gable, a cross proclaims the Christian message to all pilgrims this way come. The rest of the building is a real hodgepodge of architectural styles. The monks clearly undertook their work in stages. Norman windows give way to Gothic forms, early Gothic giving way to their successors. It may well be possible to study this building alone and come away with a rudimentary knowledge of medieval English church architecture as a whole.

During the Reformation, the Priory became a village parish church. Much was changed and torn down, but worship and community life continued. This long story was at risk of coming to an end a decade or so ago when parishioner numbers fell to such a low level it was thought the church had become unsustainable. Thankfully, a trust was formed from courageous and enthusiastic locals, recognising the importance of St Germans to them and to the country. Their aim is 'to return this important building and surrounding grounds into an effective community resource as well as retaining it as a place of worship.' I encourage all who can to visit and support the work of the St Germans Priory Trust. And there will be many. St Germans marks the beginning of a new 125-mile pilgrimage route, the Cornish Celtic Way, across the county to St Michael's Mount.

Dore Abbey, Abbey Dore Herefordshire

Dore Abbey is as evocative a memorial to monastic England as I can remember seeing. An imposing spread of deep red sandstone is easily counterbalanced by the grand sweep of Herefordshire's Golden Valley. It is easy to see why the Cistercians arrived here in 1147 to found their religious house. Favouring an ascetic interpretation of the Rule of Benedict, emphasising simplicity, austerity and hard physical labour, it is somehow apt for such an order to have made it to a spot that remains supremely tranquil and productive to this day.

What is now a parish church is entered through the south transept of the former monastery. At first this can be confusing; the arrangement is so high, so domineering, yet at the same time somehow jumbled together. This is until the west end of the church is viewed and the roofline of what was once a huge 175 ft-long nave is visible. Vast as it remains, Dore Abbey is only a surviving fragment of the spiritual citadel raised between the final decades of the twelfth century and the dawn of the thirteenth.

An array of tall, narrow lancet windows crowned by pointed arches mark the transition of this building away from what would be roughly considered Norman architecture. Concurrent to this observed architectural change the underlying structures of Norman identity were also beginning to shift. By this stage, the third generation of

Anglo-Normans were being raised on lands occupied at the Conquest. Intermarriages were common, local saints adopted, a new assimilated English identity was emerging alongside the bulwark of Henry II (1133–89; r.1154–89), the first Plantagenet king of England.

Pointed arches are distinctive and easily separate what can be viewed as the Gothic from the round arches associated with Norman or Anglo-Saxon structures. This is criminally simplistic and in a great many cases untrue. Nevertheless, a broad pattern exists. Yet it is the architectural possibilities opened up by this step forward in structural engineering that really unlocks what came to be known as the 'Gothic'. Now there's space and light in volumes as yet unseen.

This can be experienced under the crossing of Dore Abbey. Those big transept arches allow for a great play of light and space, ushered in through the equally monumental lancet windows. At the east end, a decorative geometric precision is displayed, if constructed but a few decades earlier.

After its suppression in 1536, Dore Abbey came into the possession of the Scudamore family. Following nearly a century of decay, in the 1630s, the family eventually paid for the choir and transepts to be restored for the use of the local parish. Lush polished seventeenth-century carpentry now adorns the early Gothic interior, well worth seeing

even without the architectural wonders that frame these decorative adornments.

Leaving Dore Abbey just after I had visited Kilpeck, I was aware of the changes in architectural form from the beginning of the twelfth century to the end. It, therefore, might seem strange to see the abbey appear in this section on the Conquest of the Normans. For me, the abbey was the church building to pivot around as I assembled my chronology of English church architecture, crude though that may seem to some readers.

St Mary the Virgin, Iffley Oxfordshire

Anyone who visits Oxford should take a walk up the Thames and over Iffley lock to the great Norman church of St Mary the Virgin. It's a lovely stroll and in a city of architectural splendour still counts as among its finest and most underappreciated of achievements. The last time I saw Iffley I came the other way at the end of a long walk up the Thames Path from somewhere near Maidenhead.

Built in the 1160s, the church remains essentially as it was when first designed, save the chancel partly rebuilt in the thirteenth century and a few other relatively minor alterations. First, we come to the great west front baring its plethora of zig-zag chevrons like the teeth of some extinct Jurassic sea beast. Three arched windows with pillars and capitals stand above a large round window – replaced by the Victorians but true to the original design – and the west doorway features a double row of menacing 'beakheads', symbols of the zodiac and the four evangelists, as well as, of course, chevrons galore. The small, but arguably more impressive, south doorway carries the same symbolic importance. Medieval lives may have been fearsomely short but they were pregnant with meaning.

The nave has two great semi-circular tower arches. It's worth noting the sophisticated use of inset Tournai marble shafts, imported from what would be modern-day Belgium. This is another sign of the evolution of architectural styles and the crude but necessary categorisations we make. A stained-glass nativity window by artist John Piper (1903–92) is a real highlight, placed in a richly carved Norman window. The addition of the thirteenth-century chancel adds a touch of daring and drama to the east end. There is also a superb thirteenth-century Lamb of God carving, discovered in the rector's garden in the 1960s and now rehoused in the church.

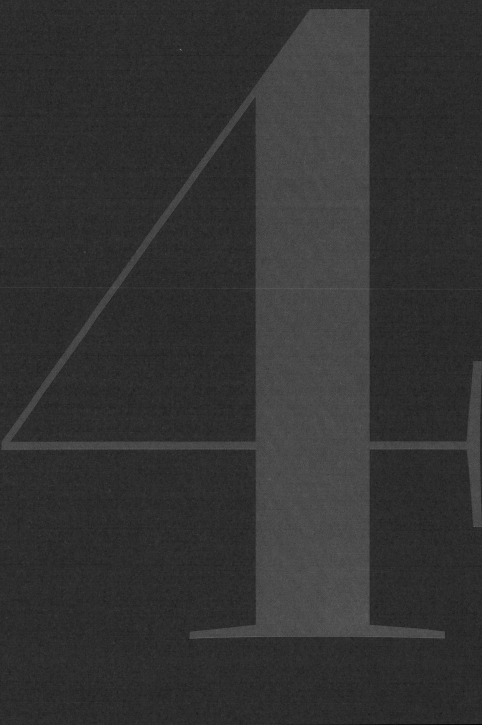

The Gothic in England

A National Architectural Style Emerges

These buildings represent some of our greatest achievements. They tell our story – soul, brain and muscle. Spreading from an experimental base in the abbeys of northern France, the Gothic style had arrived in England by the mid-twelfth century; initiating a 400-year quest for volume and light. The thrusting solid power of Anglo-Norman architecture slowly morphed into gently pointed arches, refined piers and high vaults.

The Gothic in England didn't simply recreate French engineering and artistry. The approaches began to be ameliorated and massaged into distinct architectural styles, as the masons of England got to work on thousands of church building projects. In 1817, these styles were categorised by the antiquarian church crawler Thomas Rickman (1776–1841) as Early English (1175–1250), Decorated (1250–1350), and Perpendicular (1350–1540). Rudimentary, perhaps, but these categorisations have endured. If they are taken as loose guides, we can happily use them to explore the elaboration of England's glorious medieval church buildings.

St Mary the Virgin, West Walton Norfolk

An out-of-the-way village clinging to the westerly edge of Norfolk, the Church of St Mary the Virgin is in possession of one of the best examples of English early Gothic architecture in the country. The detached bell tower at West Walton, was constructed around 1240 and represents the high summit of this first flourishing of Gothic building work in England. At the base, it opens on all sides with arches guarded by some robust looking niches. Above, the eye is drawn to a stage of magnificent arcaded lancets, the icons of the age – slender and simple early Gothic openings with a pointed arch. Still higher, the tower extends upwards before a parapet and pinnacles from the fifteenth century.

Out on the surrounding flat marshlands, the tower promises to draw the visitor towards a far larger structure, a cathedral perhaps. The church some 60-ft or so away is also built in the Early English style but externally lacks the confidence the masons of England had found elsewhere, or would do so in subsequent decades. It is low and flat. No doubt those who constructed this building didn't trust the ground enough to directly attach such a monstrous tower – there were other examples where a hefty tower pulled and warped the main structure of a church into a ruinous state due to subsidence.

While the church might seem squat and windblown from the outside, it keeps a great secret. Inside, the sense of light and proportion immediately conveys the genius of early Gothic architecture. There is stillness and dignity here, something ineffably sacred stirred in the cool morning light. It's relatively simple, uncluttered, as churches of this style would have been. A long nave with clerestory – the upper part containing a series of windows – and a fifteenth-century timber roof provide the atmosphere of a great hall. Aisles spread out to either side and clear glass gestures in an abundance of pure soft sun. The carved foliage on the capitals of the arcades is a crisp and fresh record of the crafts nurtured in these years. How exhilarating this period must have been for the masons experimenting with new forms and structures as they groped for eternity in stone.

For me, West Walton doesn't quite achieve the comprehensive glory of the final stages of early Gothic architecture in England. Having said that, I wouldn't argue with anyone who chose such a building as their favourite. Some might say this is a simpler, purer form of early Gothic architecture, the moments of virtuoso artistic talent providing a human touch lingering in the spirit of the place.

There can be few better examples than the campanile at West Walton, if you are have an interest in thirteenth-century church architecture.

The Church of St Margaret, Little Faringdon
Oxfordshire

The old church at Little Faringdon sits just in Oxfordshire on the border with Gloucestershire. It was built in the opening decade of the thirteenth century and, as such, demonstrates some transitional features between the Anglo-Norman and Early English architectural styles. While the heavily moulded arches of the nave arcade are still rounded and the piers circular, unadorned, the capitals above murmur with a naturalistic treatment to the stone – the sprouting of 'stiff leaf' foliate carvings which emerged around this time as lush additions to church architecture. The contrast with earlier 'flat leaf' carvings, is almost as if to observe the transition from black-and-white to colour television. Where once there were outlines, gestures, indications, suddenly there is movement, depth, energy. While the capitals here don't quite showcase the full bloom of this development, they are a wonderful example of how such architectural forms have moved on.

The plain and simple pairs of lancet windows on the north aisle indicate the epic search for light to unfold in the coming centuries. As it is, these windows, contemporary with the majority of the early thirteenth-century nave, allow in but a little light and, thus, there is still a somewhat gloomy feel to the interior. This pattern is repeated in the chancel which also has a pair of lancets at the east end with dainty hood moulding on the exterior. One of England's finest twentieth-century chroniclers of medieval ecclesiastical architecture, Frank Ernest Howard (1888–1934), points to this as 'an untouched Early English chancel'. Perhaps that is so, in a quiet unassuming sense. Still, the twinkling is here in those carved capitals, in the work that must have been invested in those mouldings, of the great explosion in Gothic architecture to come.

Hexham Abbey, Hexham Northumberland

This monumental building is perhaps best known for its Anglo-Saxon origins, including the crypt, which remains from the church of St Wilfrid (c.633–c.709/10) founded here in the seventh century. Made Bishop of Northumberland after a six-year odyssey to Rome, he became a pupil of Boniface (c.675–754), Wilfrid sponsored several ambitious construction projects. At Hexham, there was a ready supply of stone available from a nearby ruined Roman fort. A fragment of an altar to Maponus Apollo, a hybrid Romano-Celtic object of veneration, can still be seen embedded in the ceiling of one of the crypt passages.

Remarkably, St Wilfrid's 'frith' stool also survives in the centre of the choir, an object over 1,300 years old, carved from a single block of sandstone and smoothed by a multitude of haunches down the ages. It was to the frith stool that a person seeking the right of sanctuary would have headed; the quintessence of spiritual authority set against the lesser Earthly jurisdiction of men. 'Frith' is Anglo-Saxon in origin and has been loosely translated as meaning 'security' and 'peace'. Unsurprisingly, it's this stool and the associated stories of St Wilfrid that so often make for the thumb fodder of our social media age – and rightly so. And yet other wonders await the visitor to Hexham Abbey.

Those entering the abbey step into the south transept, beside the time-worn romance of the night stair, used by monks as they dragged themselves from the sweet release of sleep back into a demanding cycle of prayer. Ahead of them is the north transept and six tall, lancet windows carved in the thirteenth century. These form a truly stunning spectacle. Sadly, the original glass is long gone – replaced in 1837 with the inoffensive and colourful set we see today. Framed by blind arcading below and these massive windows above, we get a distinct sense of the transformative atmosphere the early Gothic masons were attempting to realise. At some eight centuries distance, even the harshest critic would have to agree that they at least partially achieved their goals here at Hexham.

There are so many further treasures in this remarkable building, beyond the crypt and frith stool. Highlights include panel paintings in the chancel, the late fifteenth-century Leschman screen, with associated carvings, and the eighth-century 'Acca's Cross'. Yet for the architectural historians the lancets aren't to be forgotten. They are the paragons of an age – the potent, vigorous, uncluttered manifestations of a new architectural language.

The Church of St Margaret of Antioch, Stoke Golding Leicestershire

Apocryphal or not the tale is too enticing to shy away from ... So, it's said, on 22 August 1485, the villagers of Stoke Golding, in Leicestershire, clambered up the tower of their church to watch over the Battle of Bosworth Field. Below, the fate of the realm would be decided. Yorkist king Richard III (1452–85; r.1483–5) was slain and Lancastrian contender Henry Tudor, the future Henry VII (1457–1509; r.1485–1509) victorious. A dynasty born in a Leicestershire field watched from a church tower.

As I walked into the churchyard at Stoke Golding a kind gentleman asked if I needed any help. He was there to assist someone completing topographic surveys for a monument which will soon commemorate the famed battle which drew a line under the Wars of the Roses. When I mentioned my interest in the thirteenth and fourteenth century Gothic architecture of the church, he was thrilled. I was directed to the guidebooks bursting with agreeable comments from a range of experts laid out before me. I didn't disagree with them.

The interior here is stunning. As beautiful a Decorated Gothic church as I have seen. The late thirteenth century four-bay nave arcade is what I'd come to see, from which a cast of heads emerge from foliage on the capitals of shafted piers – one

of those characters apparently suffering from toothache.

The window tracery on the south side of the church plays a tremendous role in enlarging the interior. Observing the tracery of these windows, there can be little doubt they represent an elaboration of the early Gothic style, certainly in comparison to what is commonly termed the Early English. However, the full flowing organic feel the Decorated Gothic is renowned for hadn't quite arrived – certainly not to the same extent as the carved pillars and the oak leaf carvings.

There is an important detail though.

One window alone on the south side of the church has curved ogee tracery, at the far eastern end. It searches for something other than those around it. Why is that? Were the masons made aware of developments elsewhere and asked to experiment? The ogee, sometimes known as 'the line of beauty', anticipates a more sophisticated 'curvilinear' Gothic: the archetypal Decorated Gothic-style which disrupts geometric assemblages in place of cusping, curves and shadow play as part of a complex whole.

All this goes to show that the academic debates on architectural forms will continue interminably as detailed observation begets detailed observation and arbitrary demarcations crumble into philosophical dust. Yet perhaps it's enough to say this is a beautiful church. Certainly, that it demonstrates a particular period in Gothic church architectural development is secondary to the warm feeling I left with, one no doubt augmented by the rich harvest festival displays the local community had put on show.

St Cuthbert, Fishlake South Yorkshire

The twelfth-century Romanesque south doorway is so often the celebrated feature at the Church of St Cuthbert at Fishlake. With four orders of intricate carving to convey the history of salvation, this is unsurprising. The praise is gushing. Alas, I must say I probably swept through this acclaimed threshold all too quickly. I had another reason for visiting.

That reason was the fourteenth-century decorated Gothic east window. I had been made aware of its existence by the aficionado of Yorkshire churches and long-standing enthusiast of all things Decorated Gothic, Rob Andrews, so much so I needed to see it for myself. In truth, I'd never quite appreciated Decorated Gothic architecture as much as people like Rob. My taste is firmly late Gothic, nurtured across the wealthy wool belt of England, from Somerset to Norfolk, where church building reached an astonishing crescendo in the late fifteenth century. At Fishlake though, this viewpoint was strikingly amended. I stood in the morning light before a shimmering ethereal vision, dumbstruck by the genius of those who first installed this wonder.

With seven lights of curvilinear tracery there appears to be more glass than wall at the end of a dazzling chancel. Everything here is so delicate. Walking towards this masterpiece it was almost as if the stonework shifted in the breeze, so graceful were the fingers spread out above me. And, finally, I got it. I understood what the Decorated Gothic was all about and why so many held a deep affection for such work. The power of this window has been lifted by a restoration which I note occurred in 2001. Sadly, I can't find further details of that work or who undertook it.

Those who did so are to be praised.

St Andrew, Heckington Lincolnshire

It's a wonder to stand before the 'Easter sepulchre' at St Andrew's church, in Heckington, and imagine ourselves moving through the solemn late-medieval Holy Week ceremonies. Palm Sunday processions initiated this ritual cycle, native yew branches held in place of the palms waved at Christ's entry into Jerusalem. From the church, the faithful filed to a temporary churchyard cross, awaiting the Blessed Sacrament – the bread and wine representing the body and blood of Christ. At the west door a fever pitch of emotion rose as the chancel veil, in place since the start of lent, was raised. The people fell to their knees for Mass.

All through that week candles would have burned before the Easter sepulchre, a stone canopied niche or wooden frame placed in the north chancel incorporating a flat recess to receive the consecrated Host – the unleavened bread of the Sacrament. On Good Friday, the Host would have been raised into the sepulchre in a small metal pyx – a highly decorated metal container. This was placed within the sepulchre alongside a crucifix bundled in linen. As the incense and chanting settled a watch took position to guard the buried Host in the pit of the sepulchre. All through the nights, church officers sat and waited until Easter Sunday and the removal of the Host and crucifix.

St Andrew's sepulchre dates from the first half of the fourteenth century and is one of the best remaining examples in England. Most have been lost. Demonstrating the ritual intensity of Holy Week, we see the small recess to receive those venerated objects. At the top are two angels beneath the risen Christ. At the base, Roman soldiers guard the tomb. Either side are panels of St Peter and the Three Marys. All is framed by decorative foliage.

Before I'd reached the Easter sepulchre, I admired the building's exterior. Rebuilt in the early fourteenth century, the church is a powerful work with clerestory, nave, aisles, transepts and chancel all sumptuously carved. The swirling, lively reticulated tracery in most of the windows, but particularly the chancel east window, can be referenced as textbook examples of the flowing Decorated Gothic style. It was the south porch that really caught my eye. While its niches have long been emptied by the industry of England's iconoclasts, it gives us a magnificent insight into the rising confidence and increased freedom of the masons working on these buildings in the fourteenth century. This is luxuriant, exuberant work at a time when rising prosperity saw a swathe of churches being rebuilt.

As this construction work took place the porches of England were invested with the commensurate resources to beautify these proud spiritual thresholds. Within a twisting display of scroll work, we find heraldic shields, angels bent in praise and the surmounting figure of Christ – although this appears to be a later substitution. The thick stonework and festival of carvings imbued with meaning would have been a powerful statement – this is a shelter and the entrance to the divine realm beyond.

Collegiate Church of Holy Trinity, Tattershall Lincolnshire

It was in the traumatic aftermath of the Black Death that a truly English architectural style emerged. This is the Perpendicular Gothic. For me, this style of church is the guiding icon of the English countryside, the steady unerring sentinel of home. In the thrusting mullions and pinnacles of the 'perp', we can locate an architecture of the people, of guilds and merchants, of practical minds searching for lightness and grace. Where the wool and weaving industries were strongest, it almost seems as if the churches of whole counties were transformed in a cacophony of hammering and chiselling, as prosperous patrons feverishly searched for the eternal protection of their souls in an England dominated by religion. East Anglia, the Cotswolds, Somerset and Devon. A certain idea of England was constructed under the Gothic towers of these churches.

Yet, the collegiate church at Tattershall is in Lincolnshire – home to the grandest Perpendicular Gothic church in a county known for the quality of its ecclesiastical architecture. It was built under the patronage of the fabulously wealthy Ralph Cromwell (c.1393/94–1456), veteran of Agincourt and lord high treasurer to the young king, Henry VI (1421–71; r.1422–61, 1470–1). As such, it eschews some of the characteristics I have outlined above. However, having been constructed alongside the famed red brick Tattershall Castle, it does capture so much of the essence of Perpendicular Gothic.

Stepping into the nave through the charming wicket gate of the porch, there is an abundance of height and volume. Moving forward, it is the chancel that best captures the shimmering sea of glass which the Perpendicular is known for. To either side are five huge windows with the characteristic straight mullions cut by the horizontal transoms. The verticality of the assemblage draws us ever upwards.

There are dozens of differing tales as to what happened to the original stained glass here at Tattershall, but all agree that in the eighteenth century a vicar requested it be removed to lighten the church. This move was met by outrage, but one night much of the glass was indeed removed. Subsequently, there was a dispute about the costs for the new clear glass and much of the chancel was bricked up for a time. All that remains today of the original stained glass is to be found in the east window, either surviving the purge or having been later reinstalled. But what decorative impact must have been conveyed as warm twilight descended through an entire church of such glass.

Priory Church of St Mary the Virgin, Steeple Ashton Wiltshire

Wiltshire once prospered from wool and broadcloth. Between 1475 and 1550, the trade in cloth between London and Antwerp doubled. Merchants in London would give credit to their networks in the regions, the tentacles of pan-continental trade reaching deep into the English countryside. Wool was the backbone of the medieval English economy. I've read many stories of Flemish and Italian merchants visiting such places, even marrying into local communities.

And much of the wealth from this trade poured into the churches of England; the great Perpendicular Gothic 'wool churches', such as this one: St Mary's, Steeple Ashton, Wiltshire. They represent the dynamism of international trade, the faith and spiritual insurance policies of the local grandees, and the majesty of late medieval stone masons.

Robert Long and Walter Lucas were both clothiers who left substantial sums for the aisles of the church to be rebuilt in the final years of the fifteenth century, while the parishioners covered much of the other costs – save the tower, which is thought to date from the first part of the fifteenth century.

The results of these spiritual investments were spectacular. Seventy pinnacles pierce the sky and twice the number of external carvings, gargoyles and grotesques, leer over the churchyard. Steeple Ashton will always be one of my favourite examples of the Perpendicular Gothic architectural style. Approaching from the nearby fields the church provides an almost fantastical vision, a fairy-tale structure for any approaching pilgrim to gaze upon. To walk towards it through the dawn mist is an unforgettable experience.

Around half the churches that existed in England at the time of the Reformation were built in the preceding five decades, in this broad style. On a quiet day, churches like this allow us to imagine the civic theatre and ritual that would have surrounded late medieval English religion: the sensory overload of flickering candlelight over vivid decoration, incense in the air, guilds and feast days giving rhythm to the year.

The interior rivals the exterior explosion of Perpendicular Gothic pinnacles. Here we have exquisite lierne (short rib) vaulting forming a high web above. Light beams in through the clerestory. This is the elevated sensory spectacle of the late medieval church.

The spire at Steeple Ashton was struck by lightning in July 1670. Faithfully, the structure was repaired before being struck again in October. This time the damage was worse, taking out a good part of the nave and aisles as it came crashing down. It wasn't replaced.

St Mary the Virgin, Berkeley Gloucestershire

At Berkeley, I walked carefully, almost reverently, round the back of a leaf blown and ramshackle churchyard. It's moments like this that stick in my memory, that call me back to the ancient places. You never quite know what you'll find when exploring an ancient church.

Beside the infamous castle where Edward II (1284–1327; r.1307–27) was murdered, I stopped at a delicate Perpendicular Gothic doorway. It would have been so easy to miss. *Thieves beware*, said the little blue and yellow sign on the window. Built in the mid-fifteenth century, in the church an elaborate ogee crocketed arch marked the threshold into the Berkeley family chapel. The family arms held by a pair of proud, watchful angels.

Inside are the remains of James, 11th Lord Berkeley (c.1394–1463) who built the chapel. Subsequent members of the family lie in rest here, too. Still owned by the Berkeley family, the chapel continues as the mausoleum to one of England's oldest noble lineages – one of only three English families that can trace their patrilineal descent back to Anglo-Saxon times.

The bell tower at St Mary's is detached from the body of the church. The early Gothic west front, with five tall lancet windows, is a sublime example of such work. Inside is more early Gothic architecture and some classic 'stiff leaf' capitals on the arcades. There are some strange carvings up there, including two women chatting

beneath a toad. A remarkable alabaster effigy memorialises Thomas, 8th Lord Berkeley (c.1326–61) and his second wife, Lady Katherine (d.1386) – two angels in attendance. Thomas fought alongside his brother at the Battle of Crecy in 1346. But for me, the wonder of Berkeley was this little Perpendicular doorway at the back of the church.

If pushed, I would go so far as to say, I think it might be my favourite portal in England.

St Mary the Virgin, Isle Abbotts Somerset

This is deepest Somerset where a rich ham stone church tower draws towards it all the dozing beauty of a quiet, ancient village. On the summer day I visited, only the buzz of insects could be heard. One of the residents came out to tend their garden and proudly tell me about the church. It dates back to the thirteenth century, while the Perpendicular Gothic tower was added around 1510. Remarkably, ten of the original statues in the tower survived the chaos of the Reformation, civil war and everything between and since. What a rare and valuable building this is.

I visited on a day off during a particularly stressful period in my life. How needed it was to chat with a local, then potter among the remote stillness of this sleepy parish. I now view this church as a sort of noble friend – dignified, calming and worthy of my respect.

Inside, the carved bench ends are late medieval and the pulpit Jacobean. Barrel roofed and strikingly high, the chancel is punctuated by a simple five-light east window. There is a bedragoned Norman font which has to be seen. Yet the carvings on the tower are the main event. The Virgin and Child and the Resurrection I found mesmerising. This is a place that's always hard to leave.

'It's pretty well tucked away up here', the man I'd spoken to had said. And indeed, it is. Down winding lanes that give out onto wide open fields, Isle Abbotts is well worth seeking.

St Mary the Virgin, Woolpit Suffolk

I once had a fever for double-decker porches.
It's a strange thing to say. But it is so. Such
maladies have from time to time led me to
not unpleasant villages such as Woolpit,
somewhere in the middle of Suffolk.
Here I found some fine East Anglian flint
checkerboard flushwork on an imposing
fifteenth-century south porch. Built through
the generosity of a series of bequests, there
is so much to admire about this porch.
Thinking back, it's perhaps here, at Woolpit,
that I firmly pinned myself to the banner
of 'the perp'.

The porch is remarkably high, with the
quatrefoils on the parapet standing proudly
above the line of the south aisle. High
up there on the crown a host of intricate
carvings dazzle, decorative fireworks to
make a mockery of anyone who thinks
the Perpendicular Gothic formulaic. An
endearing little stairway turret, tucked in the
northwest corner, would have once led weary
legs up to the parvise, or upper chamber,
where documents would have been stored or
perhaps a priest would have slept – how many
scenes I have conjured up in my mind's eye of
the windblown nights which must have been
spent in such spaces.

On the frontage, a whole series of
elaborate niches rise over a gorgeous ogee
doorway. It seems work on this porch took
many decades, perhaps starting as early as the
1420s and was not finished until the middle
of the 1470s when the rector, John Lynton,
gifted the fat sum of £20 so that statues could
be placed in those niches. Of course, those
statues are long gone, but the visual impact
of the overall assemblage endures.

Squires and Parsons

Georgian England

The Georgian era saw a succession of four Hanoverian kings, all
named George, between 1714 and 1830, and strangely ended with
one named William, who reigned until 1837. It seems an arbitrary
demarcation and yet, sandwiched between the turmoil of the
seventeenth century and the industrial accelerants of Victorian
society, there is something instantly recognisable about the
Georgian. When it comes to church building, this sentiment is
translated into a refreshed and stylistically diverse architectural
language. Yet still, it is enough to see a building from this period
and you can usually give a knowing nod and murmur, 'Georgian'.
It was a time of experimentation and refinement, of rising
prosperity and a confident Britain emerging as a global power.

It is easy to slip into the gentle, peaceful image of the
Georgian parish reflected in the ordered social hierarchies
of draught-proofed box pews beneath the steady gaze of the
Royal Arms. However, this was also a time of emboldened
nonconformism, of Methodism and simmering social
malcontent. Against this backdrop, I have found exploring
the Georgian churches of England to be a deeply enriching
experience. I see this as the great time of country squires and
parsons, in close union with the state, striving to maintain
their vision of orderly Anglican life in a rapidly changing and
increasingly outward-facing Britain.

St Mary Magdalene, Croome D'Abitot Worcestershire

The original church at Croome was demolished by George, the 6th Earl of Coventry (1722–1809), when he decided to replace his adjacent Jacobean house in the 1750s. The new house and park were designed and laid out by influential landscape architect 'Capability' Brown (c.1715–83), as was the church, set on a low hill as an 'eye catcher' in warm Bath stone.

When I visited, the air was fresh and the light radiant. The views over the Malvern Hills, spectacular. Above the parkland and the great neo-Palladian mansion – Croome Court – it was still. Little has changed here since the church was consecrated in 1763.

Interestingly, the church was originally sketched by Brown in the Classical style, fronted by a columned portico. At some point this design was sidelined. Today, we see an early Gothic revival tower on the hillside, demonstrating the contested architectural ideas of the age. The interior is sumptuous. Perhaps no surprise, as Robert Adam (1728–92) was brought in to design it. From plaster mouldings to an outlandish wine-glass pulpit, some of the finest craftsmen of the age went to extraordinary lengths to render Adam's vision a reality. Here, too, we find the importance of *the Word* to eighteenth-century Anglicans, as expressed in a highly decorated Commandment board.

Adam's work is a fitting frame for the lavish Coventry monuments transferred from the old church. Here the family elders recline in glory beneath sweeping canopies. At times these figures are actually quite comical to the modern viewer, though the artistry on display is clear.

The family lived at Croome until 1949. After they departed, a dwindling congregation struggled on for some years until the church was declared redundant in 1973. St Mary's is now in the care of the Churches Conservation Trust, while Croome Court is cared for by the National Trust.

St Mary, Old Dilton Wiltshire

I adore Georgian church interiors like this. There is something homely and warm about them, so different in tone to the medieval buildings they often sit within. The fourteenth-century St Mary's rests on a country lane not so far from Westbury and its famous White Horse. It's not the most beautiful exterior but nor is it offensive. The little stone spire is amusing, even cute. But it is the interior that calls the church botherers to this unassuming place.

After collecting the old key from a nearby house, you unlock St Mary's and enter the carpentered elegance of the eighteenth century. Box pews line the nave, medieval timbers somewhere in the mix. A three-decker pulpit with canopy dominates the south wall. If you ever visit, just look at the exquisite bannister leading up to the top tier. This central arrangement speaks of the emphasis on sermons in the eighteenth century. Often these would have been lengthy affairs. The Word of God needed to be heard and understood. It should be remembered this was a time when the likes of John Wesley (1703–91) were preaching to tens of thousands in headline open-air performances. While there must have been tedium among the pews at times, it would be a mistake to see the gentility of Georgian furnishings as reflecting the religiosity of those who worshipped here. This was a time of intense faith, nurtured in a renewed fashion.

Another charming touch at St Mary's is the gallery north of the chancel, once used as a schoolroom and complete with its own fireplace. From the gallery, you look down on an ordered church, finely produced, to harmonious effect.

St John, Westminster Greater London

I found myself working for the luxury fashion house Burberry during my early to mid-twenties. As a shy boy, this was a bit of a nightmare. At lunch, I would scurry past the towering fashionistas out into the streets of Westminster. For a heavenly half hour, I would nose a book on the steps of St John's, in nearby Smith Square. It became my sanctuary, my refuge of calm from the corporate cut and thrust of Horseferry House.

Lounging on a square just away from the political centre of Westminster Palace and Millbank, this magnificent church was tragically firebombed during the Second World War. Thankfully, it found new life and was restored as a concert hall in the 1960s. Inside, striking white Corinthian columns hold up the roof, while scarlet curtains and wooden galleries rise over a chequerboard floor. It is all primed and ready for performance and theatre. Regarded as one of the finest examples of English Baroque architecture, the building forms a centrepiece to this intimate and evocative slice of London. How thankful we must be to those who rescued this from a smouldering ruin to the cultural institution it is today. The view of St John's down the contemporary brick houses of Lord North Street conjures up one of the iconic images of early Georgian London.

St John's was built in 1728 as one of fifty planned new Churches. With the increased religious freedoms first ushered in by the Toleration Act (1689), it eventually became apparent to the government that in a rapidly expanding London, new church buildings were needed so as to maintain the supremacy of the Anglican faith. In 1711, the Commission for Building Fifty New Churches was established with the mandate to build fifty churches, funded by an enhanced coal tax. The commission never realised its goal, but it did build a number of notable ecclesiastic places of worship, which would become known as the Queen Anne Churches. These buildings are the product of the complex of religious currents of eighteenth-century England.

Legend has it that when Thomas Archer (c.1688–1743) was designing St John's, he asked Queen Anne how she'd like the church to look. Flipping over a footstool, she remarked, 'like that'. Ever since, the building has been known as 'Queen Anne's Footstool'. Yet, the footstool hasn't always been appreciated.

While trained in continental architecture, Archer is often seen as the lesser of his great contemporaries, John Vanbrugh (1664–1726) and Nicholas Hawksmoor (c.1661–1736). In *Our Mutual Friend*, writer Charles Dickens was particularly scathing, describing the church as 'some petrified monster, frightful, and gigantic, on its back with its legs in the air'. This seems a little harsh. Baroque is far from my favourite architectural style and yet the footstool will always have a dear place in my heart.

St Mary Woolnoth, City of London Greater London

St Mary Woolnoth was designed by architect Nicholas Hawksmoor (c.1661–1736). It is an unusual church, the tower quite unlike any other. From the front it's broad and imposing, but look from the side and it is slim, narrow. Four columns give the impression of two separate towers; a spectacle reinforced by two small turrets. A short distance from Bank, the church can be found at the junction of Lombard Street and King William Street, surrounded by some of the great institutions of the City. What a strange and valuable structure it is. Only the inimitable mind of Hawksmoor could have produced such a thing.

It was built between 1716 and 1727, another Queen Anne church. The previous church had partly survived the 1666 Great Fire of London but was in need of considerable restoration. The decision was eventually taken for Hawksmoor to entirely replace the problematic medieval structure. While today it is constrained by the corporate power of the City's swaggering powerbrokers, a print from 1838 shows St Mary Woolnoth when it still dominated the cityscape. When walking past the church, I stare at that big black octagonal clock face with its gold numerals, as referenced in T. S. Elliot's masterpiece 'The Waste Land'.

What worlds have come and gone on these city streets. A Starbucks has attached itself to the building now. Another coffee hut resides in the entranceway. If you ever find yourself at Bank station, you can pick up a hot drink and head inside. Here is a refined world, a place of quiet and calm, gently insulated from the chaos outside. Clean, crisp and powerful Corinthian columns hold together a structure inhabited by rich plasterwork and gorgeous inlaid and polished wood.

St James, Stanstead Abbotts Hertfordshire

I trudged through the mists of the Lea Marshes to reach this old church. Welcoming visitors is a charming fifteenth-century porch. I sheltered from the rain under its mighty timbers before starting out on my return journey, as so many must have done down the centuries. There is an acute satisfaction to be found in sharing these simple and repeated patterns of behaviour. The melody of the rain, the shiver of the wind, the raindrops mindlessly caught by the stroke of a forefinger on hewn wood. They, too, would have known such things.

Inside is a Georgian gem. Box pews throughout and a proud three-decker pulpit in the middle of the nave. The main fabric of the building is much older, dating back to at least the twelfth century and most likely replacing previous structures on the site. It is even thought by some that Roman brick or tile has been integrated into the flint and rubble walls in places. Yet in atmosphere this is an eighteenth-century delight; a place that conveys the social hierarchies of an England set on maintaining and refining its class structures.

Elsewhere in the interior, there is some charming brass, including a little unknown knight, a dog faithfully looking up at his feet. Dominating the north chapel, is the late seventeenth century Baesh monument where Sir Edward and wife face each other, kneeling in prayer. A modern touch is provided by Thomas Denny whose precious stained glass works are some of the glories of England's religious buildings. This piece was commissioned by Catherine Joan Trower in memory of her husband, Anthony (1921–2005). In varying shades of blue, purple and cyan,

two lights have been fitted. Based on Psalms 37 and 84, a pair of figures gaze at a paradise ahead on the left, while on the right is an ambiguous depiction: a figure surrounded by their papers, a calming mountain landscape in the distance. It is typical Denny. Bold, emotionally charged, touching, and open to interpretation. Finding one of these works is always a great pleasure.

St James is now in the care of the Churches Conservation Trust.

St Giles, Wimborne St Giles Dorset

St Giles is a church built in the Classical style and a dignified example of early Georgian church architecture. There has been a church in this village since at least the early thirteenth century. Yet, the church today is firmly eighteenth century in external appearance, having been almost entirely rebuilt in 1732. This is civilised England. A lane rolls before a row of low, charming seventeenth-century almshouses and the village green spreads out across the way. Then the church tower. Greensand ashlar checkerboarded by knapped flint. It provides a steadying, sympathetic bookend to this little corner of lush Dorset countryside.

I didn't know what awaited me when I first pulled into that quiet lane. I hadn't planned to visit at all, but made a quick detour when I spied the tower across the fields at the edge of Cranborne Chase. I'm so glad I did. This was to be my discovery of the great Gothic revival architect, Sir John Ninian Comper (1864–1960). Following a fire in 1908, Comper redesigned the interior. 'Completely medieval minded,' as described by John Betjeman (1906–84), he was permitted to let his imagination run riot here at St Giles.

A vast, dark, intricate screen separates nave from chancel. Above, a carved 'rood' crucifixion cross is flanked by the traditional Virgin Mary and St John, alongside two winged seraphim. It doesn't stop with this bold statement. By the time of the church was reconsecrated in 1910, Comper had installed a painted and gilded alabaster reredos, gilded test, dazzling stained glass, polished furnishings, a gallery, organ case and a piercing golden font cover consisting of eight columns supporting an elegant octagonal steeple. It is always a good idea to open a church door and see what's inside.

St Giles is lavish. Sumptuous. At times it borders on the gaudy, particularly when combined with the numerous memorials to the Ashley-Coopers, the earls of Shaftesbury; in particular, the canopied table tomb to Sir Anthony Ashley (1551–1628) with its heavy gilt decoration and Classical columns. He is notable for having served as secretary for war under Elizabeth I (1533–1603; r.1558–1603) – and introducing the cultivation of cabbages to these shores. In light of this startling fact and the blaze of virtuoso design features, I left St Giles in a daze. Somehow the interior successfully complements the eighteenth-century work and my visit to Wimborne St Giles will long remain one of my most fondly remembered and surprising church explorations.

The Place of Whispering Memories

Travels to England's Most Atmospheric Churches

Some churches are particularly resonant. Here the accretions of
each passing generation hang softly together and we
begin to imagine all the lives that have touched and been
touched by them. They possess a unique sense of atmosphere,
distilled in stone, wood and metal. There is a soft atavistic hum
to the light and shadows. I began to think of these buildings as
'the place of whispering memories'. When overwhelmed by life,
tired and run down, I often stop and book a day off because I
need to head to these places, to commune with myself and those
who've come before me. In the street-sweeping hours, I arrive
at a train station, ready to chug cross country and head out on
foot in search of that intangible something hidden in an old,
still church and the landscapes that cradle them.

St Michael, Duntisbourne Rouse Gloucestershire

I first dipped my head under the mossy, slated lychgate of St Michael's a little after dawn on a cool summer's morning. Guided by a hedge-lined path, I could see the belfry beyond, the meadowsweet scent of cut grass wandering up the valley to meet me from below. Someone must have mown the churchyard the previous evening.

Tudor tower, Saxon nave, Norman chancel. A sloping poem to the ages falling down its gentle Cotswolds hillside. I now call this my favourite church in all of England. In plots like this, the faith of a nation was kindled and sustained. Here, the architecture sits in perfect harmony with the surrounding Cotswold landscape and the woodlands shift softly in the breeze. Inside the church you find a Norman font, medieval wall paintings with charming floral patterns, choir stalls said to be brought in from a much larger monastic church, as well as seventeenth-century box pews. Yet this church is to be appreciated for its composition of features rather than any specific item of intrigue.

On a return visit, I stepped into the Norman crypt below the chancel.

Accessing mysterious spaces like this in historic English churches is always a privilege and an adventure. On my first visit, I hadn't known you could step down those few steps and be cocooned in centuries of uninterrupted gloom. There I stood, in the cool shadows, a simple room with just a single tiny lancet window overlooking the sweeping meadows and woodlands of the Dunt Valley below.

The centuries roll by on this hillside while elsewhere, at a distance, other things happen.

St Enodoc, Trebetherick Cornwall

To St Enodoc's I walked after the little ferry crossing from Padstow to Rock. Childhood memories came flooding back. Salt, ice cream, the sea breeze flapping the dogs ears, my older brothers marauding ahead. This is where the poet John Betjeman is buried. The poet. My mum would have told us. We wouldn't have cared much at the time. Though maybe a bit. This was the place he loved, she'd said. How much I can now relate to the lines of his poem 'Trebetherick'? It's one of many he wrote of this coastline.

Blessed be St Enodoc, blessed be the wave,
Blessed be the springy turf, we pray, pray to thee,
Ask for our children all the happy days you gave
To Ralph, Vasey, Alastair, Biddy, John and me.

The church is Norman in origin, 1430s in substance. Utterly charming, it sits in the dunes of the Camel Estuary. It's said that in the nineteenth century the church was blocked up by the shifting sands and the vicar had to be lowered in and, in so doing, he ensured that the church was 'open' for spiritual business. I've been to a church in Denmark where the same story was told; it has now almost fully succumbed to the dunes – just the tower still visible beneath mounds of sand.

On a sultry August day, I crossed the local golf course and entered the churchyard, paying my respects to Betjeman at his beautifully carved gravestone. The crooked and utterly charming stone spire leans adoringly towards the seascape it frames so perfectly. Inside, a flower display had been pinned to the surviving dado of the fifteenth-century rood screen. The church was rebuilt in the first half of that century, although some features remain from earlier structures. A Norman tower arch and font add to the character of this small, dark church. A little south aisle has been added to nave and chancel. An ancient Celtic Cross is propped up in the porch.

As I went on my way along the coast path to Port Isaac, I could understand why this place meant so much to Betjeman.

St Senara, Zennor Cornwall

Zennor is wild and remote, the Atlantic edge of our island, down on the Penwith Peninsula beyond St Ives. The writer D. H. Lawrence (1885–1930) completed his novel *Women in Love* here between 1915 and 1917, declaring the village *'the best place I have been'*.

Folklore and legend abound on the heather-topped granite cliffs. The legend of the Zennor mermaid is depicted in a bench end that rests in the village church, over 600 years after it was first carved. So the tale goes, a mermaid fell in love with a son of the churchwarden, Matthew Trewhella, and enticed him to follow her. The last sighting of dear Matthew was as the pair swam out to sea at nearby Pendour Cove.

Dedicated to an ancient saint, it's thought the church at Zennor is of Celtic origin and well over 1,300-years old. The structure we see today is much later though. Originally built in the twelfth and thirteenth centuries, the church saw the addition of the north aisle, porch and iconic three-stage embattled tower in the fifteenth century. It's this tower which so sweetly holds the settlement in place, below the moorland and the coast beyond. This is one of my favourite views.

In the late nineteenth century, the church was significantly restored from a reportedly dilapidated state, particularly noticeable in the curved wooden wagon roof. Parishioners have the choice of using a Gothic font with carved quatrefoils dating from around 1300, or a rough-hewn 'Norman' font found in the vicarage garden in the 1960s, which the guide thinks dates from much later. Despite the calming atmosphere, it's the mermaid of Zennor that most visitors seek out here.

The village pub, The Tinners Arms, is unequivocally one of the best in England – and, therefore, of course, the world. The claim is that in 1271 masons working on the church built the inn as a place to rest after a hard day's work. This is a story I'm inclined to believe purely because I want to.

Around Zennor is a landscape of abandoned tin mines and breathtaking coastal views. It's an escape from the world and a sanctuary allowing time to consider your place within it. One night while staying nearby, I lay in a field and watched the stars emerge as my eyes adjusted to the darkness, the thick band of the Milky Way roaming across the sky.

St Just, St Just in Roseland Cornwall

Lush and vibrant – St Just in Roseland. Here we find an exotic tidal creek beside the Fal River estuary. Palm trees, cedars and bamboo abound. At first sight it looks as if this were an Anglican Church in a former colony of the British Empire, the Lesser Antilles perhaps, not Cornwall. Returning from Australia, in 1897, the botanist John Treseder decided on St Just as the location for his experimentations in subtropical gardening. Now we find thirteenth-century early Gothic architecture framed by magnolias; gravestones emerging from ferns. As such, the churchyard has taken on an atmosphere quite unlike anywhere else I've visited. To quote Mr Betjeman again, it is 'to many people the most beautiful churchyard on Earth.'

At sunset it is utterly mesmerising to wander the paths away from the church, to hear the tranquil lapping of the water and find the old holy well nearby. It is thought members of the Celtic Church would have worshipped around that same well some 1,500 years or so ago. What scenes this little inlet must have witnessed: saints, traders and pilgrims.

While, the architecture is charming, it is the setting which undeniably steals the show at St Just in Roseland.

Watts Cemetery Chapel, Compton Surrey

I still remember opening the door to the Watts Cemetery Chapel and looking up into a firmament of lush colour bursting with beauty and soul, overpowering boldness and creative determination. Represented is the whole of creation – the Tree of Life, flowers, fruit, shells, fish, serpents, birds, beasts, man and woman, the sun, moon and stars. At the centre of the dome is a symbolic depiction of God in the form of a circle, without beginning or end. Moving down we observe four large seraphim – the highest order of angels in the celestial hierarchy – in vivid crimson. Further down are 24 winged messenger angels holding discs to represent the contrasting forces of day and night, good and evil, rest and labour, and so on. Shimmering in violets, turquoise, amaranth and vermillion, decoration is added in all directions. A swirl of playful colour rising in a darkened cocoon, proving that intention is the root of style.

Compton was where a community came together in the twilight years of the nineteenth century to create something of enduring beauty and meaning – the spirit of the Arts and Crafts movement manifested on a quiet rise in the Surrey countryside. Over 70 members of the local community worked on the Watts Cemetery Chapel, guided by the craftswoman, designer and social reformer Mary Watts (1849–1938).

She conceived and oversaw the construction of this 'miracle in terracotta', blending Celtic, Romanesque and Arts and Crafts' influences. It's a building completed with love and passion.

The exterior of this Christian mortuary chapel is decorated in clay tiles, moulded in the village. I'm sure inspiration was taken from Norman churches elsewhere in England, particularly Kilpeck in Herefordshire, also featured in this book (see pages 39–40). Mary wrote over a century ago, 'it is growing everyday less red and the green enfolds it all so beautifully now the trees are in leaf ... a sweet resting place'. That impression has now taken full effect, as mature trees surround the chapel, absorbing it into the landscape.

I followed a section of the old Pilgrims' Way out from Guildford to reach the chapel. Once adopted by those making their way cross country to the shrine of Thomas Becket at Canterbury, it now takes the form of a sunken lane in parts, where a tunnel of foliage guides the way. The past sublimated for centuries by nature at each passing footstep.

St Bartholomew the Great, City of London
Greater London

You enter St Bart's by passing under a Tudor gatehouse and through an original west doorway to the monastery founded here in the 1120s by Rahere – the enigmatic pilgrim, monk and sometime favourite of King Henry I (c.1068/9–1135; r.1100–35). The story goes that as Rahere lay delirious while on pilgrimage in Rome, he prayed for his life, vowing to found a hospital for the poor if he survived. He did survive, indeed, and on his way home St Bartholomew appeared to him. The rest, as they say, is history. And there is a lot of it.

Tucked away down the lanes and alleyways of Smithfield, the church gives few outward clues as to its stature as one of London's great medieval spaces. Though the nave and outer buildings were destroyed in 1539, thankfully the extensive four-bay Norman choir remains.

It's an astonishing interior. A great cavern where towering arches spread over ancient woodwork and shadowy passageways lay witness to a rich and storied past: the font William Hogarth was baptised in; the aisles across which the wounded Wat Tyler was dragged during the Peasants Revolt; the Lady chapel turned printing press where Benjamin Franklin once toiled. And the oriel window inserted in the early sixteenth century by Prior William Bolton (c.1450–1532) to keep watch over the monks is a wonderful touch.

To get a feeling for medieval London, I can think of no better place to send a visitor. And yet on all my many visits, it has been all but empty. I can explore the chapels and aisles alone, flickering candles dancing over gorgeous stone. Thanks be to Rahere whose elaborate Gothic tomb sits beside the sanctuary after being moved here in 1405. Look closely at the top of the monument and you will see flecks of the original medieval paintwork that would have once been used to decorate the entire piece.

St Peter, Southease East Sussex

Round tower churches are rare. Round tower churches outside East Anglia are extremely rare. This example, in Southease, East Sussex, is one of only a handful of England's 180 or so round tower churches outside of that county. It's a church worth visiting for the setting alone, along the South Downs Way, half a mile from the tiny and isolated village railway station.

The area would have been sparsely populated when the Normans arrived to inherit the chapel that was recorded on this site from the tenth century. Although the round tower was added to the pre-Conquest building, its modest proportions have been maintained. Inside, on a hot day, I sat and enjoyed the cool undisturbed air drifting over me while I gazed at the faded yet evocative thirteenth-century wall paintings, depicting New Testament scenes, as well as the fine Jacobean pulpit.

Southease is a restful place, sitting between the hubbub of the south coast and the thrall of the nation's capital. Writer Virginia Woolf (1882–1941) and her husband, Leonard (1880–1969) chose the neighbouring village of Rodmell to set up home at nearby Monk's House, a sixteenth-century weatherboarded cottage. You can still visit their house which is in the care of the National Trust. After leaving Southease, I pushed onwards up the River Ouse back to Lewes and caught the train home to London.

These are the days I always, *always* love the most.

St John, Duxford Cambridgeshire

St John's. Glorious decay and sheer charm. Though decay now arrested thanks to the work of the Churches Conservation Trust and their volunteers. The church has fast become a site of pilgrimage, and with good reason. It's such a special building. Dozing in a little village some nine miles or so south of Cambridge, it oozes atmosphere from every surface and angle. The promise of finding such places, to stand within them and inhale the passing of the ages, is what fires my passion for church crawling. And I'm not alone.

Here two Norman arches support the tower, framing the entrance to the

thirteenth-century chancel. A pair of canopied niches in the adjacent north chapel are among the finest objects I've ever thumbed my iPhone at. One of these niches features a 'Green Man' at its base. Over the warm and rich brick floor, I turn to pass wall paintings from the twelfth century to the end of the medieval period, beautiful carvings and light that shifts throughout the day in a virtuoso display.

It's the light that makes Duxford a place to return to, time and time again. The interior is unforgettable. A place where everything could be worked into a beautiful painting, and yet is never the same. From moment to moment, subtle modulations in colour and values add to the astonishing impact. I have long followed one of the fine Duxford volunteers on social media, Adrian Powter. Being able to view his photography of this place over the year always brings me a sense of calm and wonder.

I walked into Duxford from nearby Ickleton, where the church houses a beautiful set of medieval frescoes. Walking from church to church cross country you so often discover previously unknown treasures, and this fine slab of the country, along the West Anglia Main Line, is full of them.

St Peter, Walpole St Peter Norfolk

I reached Walpole St Peter on a crisp January morning. It took a fair while to find it. Ten miles west from Kings Lynn train station on a straight road, I'd thought it would be simple. In fairness, a clutch of 'Walpoles' were displayed on the satnav: Walpole St Peter, Walpole Cross Keys, Walpole St Andrew, Walpole Marsh and Walpole Highway all making an appearance. The taxi driver always got them confused, he said.

This particular region of Norfolk, I was informed, was very much marshland. To the east flows the Great Ouse at Lynn. Having shifted course in the thirteenth century, this once logical part of Norfolk became stranded, a fenny appendage cut off from the greater county.

As the taxi pulled away, I hauled my backpack on and faced the church tower, all that remained of a previous church built here around 1300. A great sea flood carried the rest away in 1337. It would take nearly a century for the 'Queen of the Marshlands' to fully emerge from the ruins. Yet in medieval church-building terms, this wasn't such a long time. Further constrained by the impact of the Black Death in 1348, most of the building work would have taken place from the 1350s through to its completion around 1425. The chancel pushes right up against the boundary of the consecrated land for maximum impact.

So as to maintain a route for circumnavigating the church during religious processions, an elegant solution was found: the high altar was raised, a passageway created beneath. This shadowy, moss-scented tunnel is affectionately known as the 'Bolt Hole'. It's this passage that provides the first clue as to how such grand churches came to be out here in marshland. Walking through it, you notice carved stone bosses hanging low and heavy from a vaulted ceiling. One of them, a sheep's head – the adored emblem of the medieval farmers and wool merchants who funded these buildings. What it must have been to walk through here and see these stone carvings illuminated as the entire village solemnly processed at Candlemas, marking the presentation of Jesus in the Temple, each year on the 2nd of February. You'd certainly have known where the money came from.

Inside, the low winter sun poured its soft light over a stadium of silvery ancient pews and beautifully carved bench ends. With the chancel rising up before you, the restrained piers and arcades, the uniform verticality of the window mullions, everything is just as you'd want it to be. If any church were to be presented as composite artwork it's this, surely?

As I explored the carvings and paintings, the churchwarden arrived to shuffle around some tables in the large separate space at the west end, before a large screen splitting the church. This used to act as a village hall of sorts, until one was finally built across the road. The screen was installed in the 1620s so as to provide a separate place for celebrations and, according to the church guide, 'so that if people became the worse for drink they would not create a mess in the main body of the church'. Welcoming me into his church, William, the churchwarden, soon had me on a tour of the highlights.

'Do you want to see it all opened out?' he asked, following up on my enthusiasm for the elaborate font cover dating back to *c*.1600, which has been described as looking like an oversized 'exotic Ottoman smoking machine'. After delicately stretching up to open out the wings of the cover, William took a step back and we both took our time to admire the craftsmanship of the piece. The font itself once displayed the seven sacraments of the Catholic Church, the visual rites guiding life in the Christian faith. It was entirely defaced, like so many were, during the Reformation, or in its aftermath. So many treasures lost.

Soon I was on my way, walking out from hushed cul-de-sacs, onwards a few miles to the neighbouring village of Tilney All Saints, and back to Kings Lynn, thereafter. Dykes, soil, pylons and the odd lone bungalow dotted the landscape as I passed. The rest was sky and the odd church tower.

St Beuno, Culbone Somerset

Culbone is an ancient place. In 1939, a standing stone was discovered shrouded in the thick woodland surrounding the church. An incised ring cross on the stone could date, it is thought, from as far back as the seventh century. St Beuno's time. Some think this stone was taken from a nearby row of Bronze Age stones forming part of an ancient trackway between Lynmouth and Porlock.

The church itself sits in a wooded hollow beside a stream, the sea crashing somewhere in the distance. A sweet, slated spire rests on a two-cell structure of nave and chancel while a little porch nuzzles up for visitors to shelter in. At 35 ft in internal length, it is the smallest, complete parish church in England. This, of course, is according to the guidebook. As is so often the case with these things, many a church lays claim to the noble title of being the smallest or largest in England. Whatever, it's a fairy-tale place.

Despite its modest size, the church has some notable features. A simple font stands on a little plinth against the south wall. Cut from a single piece of sandstone it is possible still to make out the chisel marks of those who worked its shape, 'nearly a thousand years ago,' as the sign extols. The rood screen dividing chancel and nave is perhaps from around 1400 and fifteenth-century benches survive, too, alongside a later seventeenth-century family box pew.

After I'd visited the church, I sat for a moment overlooking the consoling sea, coughing and sweating a bit, yet feeling much better for the air in my lungs and having made my Culbone pilgrimage at last.

St John the Baptist, Inglesham Wiltshire

The fields and lanes around this isolated church were flooded on my visit. Beaten back by the wind and the rain, I made my way through the little churchyard expecting the church to be locked. There's just a farm and a house or two here in Inglesham, along the upper Thames Path. The building itself gives little indication of the charm inside. Towerless and squat, I'm sure many have walked by without a second thought. Thankfully, the latch clicked and the door opened. Some kind soul must be the keyholder, dutybound whatever the weather.

The interior is an unrestored classic. We have no less a figure than designer, poet and artist William Morris (1834–96) to thank for an achingly romantic survival. Morris lived not far, downriver at Kelmscott Manor. Having decried the 'sham' restorations occurring at other churches in the vicinity, particularly at Burford, he was moved to create the Society for the Protection of Ancient Buildings (SPAB) – an organisation which continues to this day to do so much vital work in support of our built heritage. In the 1880s, SPAB raised funds to secure and protect Inglesham's future without the heavy restorations Morris so loathed. The church is now in the care of the Churches Conservation Trust.

There are layers of paint inside, generations of script and imagery going back to the thirteenth century, when the main structure of the building went up. The nave arcade pillars are topped by wonderfully crisp 'stiff leaf' capitals. That nave is now filled by an amusing jumble of seventeenth- and eighteenth-century box pews. The chancel is one of the highlights – a scarred and fragmented seventeenth-century text framing the Communion table. I couldn't make out the text but cast about on Instagram for help. Thankfully some

fellow church botherers and epigraphy experts were on hand.

The text is taken from the seventeenth-century King James Bible and 1 Corinthians 11: 23–26. Verses 25 and 26 are clearest:

25: After the same manner also he took the cup, when he had supped, saying, This cup is the new testament in my blood: this do ye, as oft as ye drink it, in remembrance of me.
26: For as often as ye eat this bread, and drink this cup, ye do shew the Lord's death till he come.

A Saxon carving of the Virgin and Child provides a further point of intrigue, the hand of the Lord blessing from above.

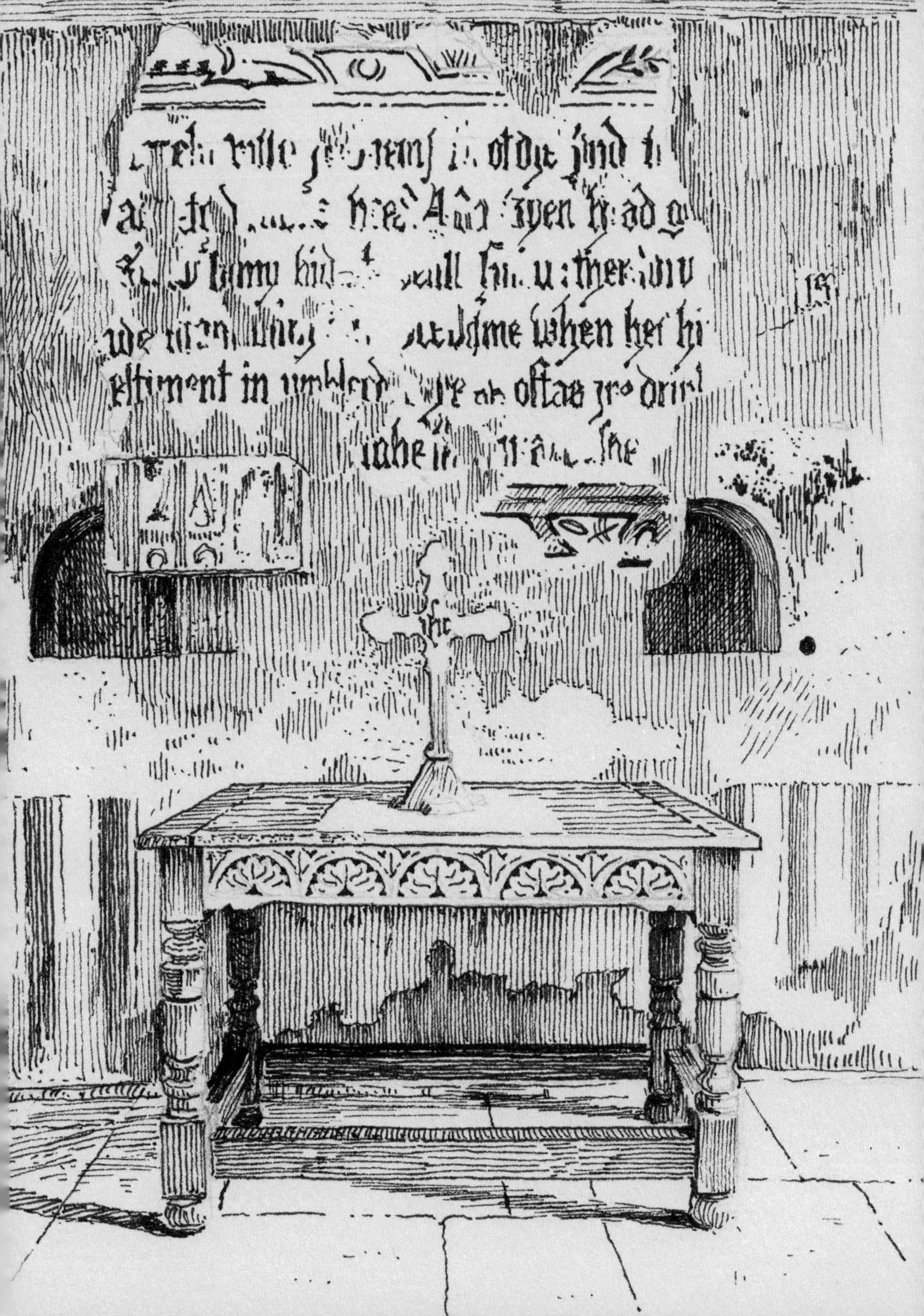

A Tumultuous Land

The Ruptures of History Writ in Stone, Wood and Metal

The scars of English history are written into the fabric of the nation's churches. However, sometimes such momentous events can be obscured from our self-conception. In 1848, continental Europe was convulsed by a series of revolutions. Britain narrowly escaped such tumult, helping give rise to the convenient view that here political institutions evolve, that we don't allow such chaos to reign. Yet England has known its uprisings too, its revolutionary moments, its civil strife and internal conflicts. To travel the churches of England is to know this. To keenly feel the emotions and trauma of a people, their courage and their bitterness, their struggles and triumphs. If we were to lose the churches of England, we would also lose a collective repository fretted with tales from, to quote Winston Churchill, this 'long island story of ours'. We can read about our history in books. These buildings, these places, allow us to step back into some of its most dramatic chapters.

All Saints, Babworth   Nottinghamshire

At Babworth, you walk down a long lane to find a handsome late medieval country church in a secluded pocket of woodland. Despite its fine proportions and bucolic setting, there is little to distinguish All Saints from any of the other parish churches of the period that frame England's thousands of villages. And yet this place *is* special, even revolutionary. It echoes the footsteps of those who would go on to play a seminal role in the settlement of the New World. On this ground, passions and convictions were kindled that would feed directly into the great American story.

In 1585, Richard Clifton (*c.1553–1616*) was appointed rector here. Clifton had studied at Cambridge, where he came under the influence of some of the most charismatic Puritan preachers of his age. In this part of the country, already a hotbed of non-conformism, he was set to stir the consciences of those who would eventually set in motion the *Mayflower* journey. This is where it began. From where William Brewster (*c.1566–1644*) and William Bradford (*c.1590–1657*) would trek to the nearby settlements of Scrooby and Austerfield to hear Clifton's words. From where a straining for freedom would lead a breakaway congregation, first to Holland and then, with an almost prophetic sense of destiny, onto the *Mayflower* and the founding of the Plymouth Colony in modern-day Massachusetts.

On my visit the church was sadly locked. I'd arrived late in the day, as dusk was deepening the greens in the surrounding trees. I sat on a bench and imagined the energy pulsing through the individuals who must have passed by where I was standing. The burning belief, the strength of faith that would lead them so far from here – from home. I didn't mind that the church wasn't open. I'd read there was a painting inside depicting the pilgrims leaving a service and also a model of the *Mayflower*. I'd have liked to see these. Yet there exists an entire network of villages around here which capture the memories of this radical time. I will have to return. There is enough in these parts for a whole book or more. For now, a glimpse into this story will suffice.

Binham Priory, Binham Norfolk

Binham Priory was dissolved in 1539, drawing to a close 450 years of Benedictine community and worship in the wilds of East Anglia. There was a time when scores of pilgrims would have been called across this landscape, into one of England's devotional heartlands. Even today the pilgrim tradition is maintained at nearby Walsingham, revered by Anglicans and Catholics alike. Yet at Binham, much of this once vast complex lies in ruins.

Thankfully, not all of the priory was laid to waste. The nave now acts as the parish church, entered via the imposing thirteenth-century west front. Although bricked up in the eighteenth century, remnants of the earliest bar tracery in Britain survive here, preceding by a few years or so the more famous examples installed at Westminster Abbey, in London, from 1245. Bar tracery was invented in French cathedrals such as Reims and Amiens during the first half of the thirteenth century and refers to windows pieced together from stone 'bars' as opposed to cutting out patterns from a plate of stone. The simplest way to think of the transition from plate tracery to bar tracery is that the stone still visually dominates the former while glass – and therefore light – dominates the latter. Those countless moments we've stood in awe contemplating the ethereal light of England's Gothic churches stem from this frontage.

Within is displayed the original rood screen dado. Whitewashed in the mid-sixteenth century, Bible texts were painted over the top. Now the figures below – saints and kings – have begun to appear again as the whitewash flakes off. These are memories of Catholic England. Indeed, an image from the Binham Priory rood dado appears on my copy of the Irish historian Eamon Duffy's *The Stripping of the Altars*, a comprehensive retelling of religion in England during the fifteenth and sixteenth centuries. The image of St Michael particularly stuck with me. How elegant and noble he looks. This is glorious High Gothic art wrapped in layers of profound social and political upheaval.

Elsewhere, a few further traces of the former priory can be seen. There is a seven sacraments font, typical of East Anglia, which has suffered but not quite been destroyed by the hands of the iconoclasts. Late medieval bench ends have been similarly brutalised, though some amusing details remain. Moving to the east end of the church, and looking back from before the altar, we can appreciate the monumental nature of these structures, not just architecturally but in terms of the overpowering psychological and economic dominance these institutions must have exerted.

This feeling is amplified when stepping out into the weeping elegiac ruins beyond. How beautiful they are, these massive broken histories.

St John the Baptist, Burford Oxfordshire

17 May 1649. Soldiers are harried up the steps, marched onto the roof of the Lady Chapel. They stare down at the churchyard. Their leaders are lined up below, held under the authority of Oliver Cromwell (1599–1658). These are the Levellers. A radical breakaway faction of the New Model Army, who've fought for parliament in the English Civil War. Now they are on the run. Mutineers, starved of pay and full of resentment for the perceived betrayal of all they hold dear – popular suffrage, religious tolerance, even experiments in economic cooperation.

Tired and hungry, five days earlier these Levellers had entered Burford to find lodgings for the night. They were on their way to rendezvous with sympathetic forces in Banbury, yet they were deceived by some in their ranks. Their location was given away. At midnight, Cromwell's cavalry burst into the town, muskets blazing. Hundreds of Levellers were able to escape into the surrounding countryside. Even so, some 340 were rounded up and locked in the church.

A war of the nerves now ensued over four days. A psychological challenge designed to break the will of these radicals. A general death sentence was teased, or a decimation – where one in ten of their number would have been killed. In these long anxiety-filled hours, one man etched his name into the lead of the church font: '*Anthony Sedley 1649 Prisner*'. These

simple words can still be seen, a tremulous memory from one of the pivotal moments in English history, where the revolutionary spirit of the English Civil War seemed to be crumpled in the tight grip of Cromwell and his mission to restore political order.

As it was, the men survived. Or at least most of them did. Three leaders of the mutiny were executed by firing squad: *Cornet Thompson, Corporal Perkins and Private Church*. A little plaque on the church wall remembers them. Many on the political left have taken these men up as martyrs and remember them in Burford each year on Levellers Day, the Saturday nearest the 17th of May.

These are the contrasts of England and its history. The green and gentle Cotswolds are where these violent scenes played out. However, even if this civil war history weren't so, the church would still be well worth a visit. A stature of the strong Norman tower is contained by spectacular fifteenth-century additions, built at a time when the local wool trade placed unprecedented wealth into the hands of the local merchant class. At this time, the nave was remodelled with vast Perpendicular Gothic windows and a clerestory inserted, alongside a glorious three-storey porch. Many a chapter could be written of this place, yet that of Anthony Sedley and his feverish scratching hands would certainly be among the most dramatic.

St Mary & All Saints, Fotheringhay Northamptonshire

If one place was to capture the dynastic drama of the Wars of the Roses, it would be Fotheringhay. Viewed from the far bank of the River Nene, the church stands as a confident example of fifteenth-century Perpendicular Gothic wealth and religiosity. Here, in bright limestone, an octagonal lantern rests on its square tower, appended by a short powerful nave of shimmering glass – a spiritual centre to command the surrounding countryside.

Once the religious foundation here was twice the size. A model in the church shows the original extent, when chancel, aisles, a west tower, cloisters, porch and other assorted buildings were in place. It was founded by Edward, 2nd Duke of York (c.1373–1415), carrying out the wishes of his father, Edmund Langley, 1st Duke of York (1341–1402). Edward wouldn't live to see the collegiate church realised. He fell at the Battle of Agincourt and was buried in the chancel, which in time would become a mausoleum to the House of York.

At the Dissolution of the Monasteries, the collegiate foundation was swept away. However, the nave, used as a parish church, was spared. Today, the east end of the church is unusually blank with just a small window above the former chancel arch. In 1566, Elizabeth I visited and saw the shattered tombs of her Yorkist forebears. Dismayed,

she made funds available for the tombs to be reinstated. These included the 2nd Duke and that of Richard of York (1411–60), the 3rd Duke, alongside his wife, Cecily Neville (1415–95).

Richard was killed at the Battle of Wakefield, in 1460, while attempting to secure his claim to the English throne. Two of his offspring, the future Yorkist kings Edward IV (1442–83; r.1461–70, 1471–83) and Richard III (1452–85; r.1483–5) would achieve his ambition. One of the most notorious figures in English history, Richard III was born at the family castle in Fotheringhay, in 1452, and in 1476, he returned the bodies of his father and his brother, Edmund (1443–60), who also fell at Wakefield, to the family church.

Those Yorkist memories loom large here. The high and short nave is adorned by various heraldic shields. Under the tower, a fan vault culminates in a falcon and fetterlock, the emblem of the House of York. A fifteenth-century pulpit, said to have been donated by Edward IV, features the white boar, white lion and black bull of the Plantagenet brothers Richard III, Edward IV and George, Duke of Clarence (1449–78). New glass for the south aisle was gifted by the Richard III Society in 1975. The 'York Window' now forms the focal point of a sort of Yorkist shrine, complete with kneelers featuring the usual symbols.

Jordans Meeting House, Jordans Buckinghamshire

It is hard to comprehend the burning passions ignited by Quakerism in seventeenth-century England. Quakers denied the Trinity and that the scriptures were the Word of God. They proclaimed they had no sin. They spoke of something called the 'spirit within'. In many ways, they inherited the radical egalitarian traditions stirred during the English Civil War. How disruptive and divisive this non-conformism must have been.

In a quiet corner of the Chilterns, we can find a window into the world of those Quakers. The Jordans meeting house dates from 1688. It was one of the first Quaker meeting houses to be purpose built, after James II (1633–1701; r.1685–8) issued his Declaration of Indulgence in 1687, permitting non-conformists to lawfully worship for the first time. It is a modest, restrained brick building. There are no architectural fireworks here. A panelled interior meets the visitor. Benches are set against clay whitewashed walls. One particularly intriguing artifact remains – a set of hat pegs. It was only when ministering that Quaker men would have taken off their hats, in ultimate deference to the Almighty. As the historian Christopher Hill puts it, 'even what seems to us the innocent eccentricity of refusing to remove the hat in the presence of social superiors, or to use the second person plural to them, confirmed conservative contemporaries in their suspicions.' In all its

unpolished humility, the meeting house can be read as a manifestation of the Quaker spirit which, before this point, would have flickered in the shadows of English life. It must have meant so much to these people to have their own place to gather.

There is little room for hierarchy or ritual at Jordans. What is here is a dedication to functional craft, a stillness of spirit, and a tremendous history. One of the founders of Quakerism, George Fox (1624–91), is recorded as having worshipped here. William Penn (1644–1718) and family are buried in the graveyard, making this a site of pilgrimage for thousands each year. After founding Pennsylvania in 1682, he would only spend another four years or so in the New World, first returning to England in 1684 and heading back to his colony between 1699 and 1701. The rest of his time was spent defending Pennsylvania from threats of Crown takeover or internal rupture, dealing with his deteriorating personal finances, and enduring a series of family crises. He died in 1718 in England with little money and his faculties long diminished. Pennsylanvia would drift away from the founding spirit of his 'holy experiment'. Yet Penn's 1682 Frame of Government would one day bleed into the ideals of democracy and liberty expressed in the American Constitution, a yearning for freedom once kindled in communities such as Jordans.

The Church of St Andrew, Mells Somerset

There's something about Mells. On the northern flank of the Mendip Hills, it's a village that whispers its colossal stories to you.

Ushered from the meadows into the churchyard by a guard of yew trees, you are transported into ancient Mells, old England. You imagine the frenzy of activity as the church was rebuilt all those centuries ago – two upper tiers of triple windows and buttress pinnacles leading up to yet more pinnacles again, a dazzling fifteenth-century creation. A bittersweet nostalgia hangs heavy.

There are so many stories to tell from this one plot of England. Yet it is the war memorial I found most poignant. Here, a marble column rises to support a sculpture of St George slaying a dragon. To either side the names of the war dead are recorded. In the centre, a panel of Portland stone bears the inscription:

WE DIED IN
A STRANGE LAND
FACING
THE DARK CLOUD
OF WAR.
AND THIS STONE
IS RAISED TO US
IN THE HOME
OF OUR DELIGHT

This memorial is by Sir Edwin Lutyens (1869–1944). The same Lutyens who created the nation's most famous war memorial, the Cenotaph on Whitehall. Indeed, his works are dotted about the village, such was his friendship with Lady Frances Horner (1854–1940), of Mells Manor.

The inscription is by Poet Laureate Robert Bridges (1844–1930). It's tremendous. These men, many of them mere boys, plucked from their villages into the machinery of continental warfare. Gamekeepers, gardeners, colliery workers alongside Edward, the last son and heir of the Horner family – which had held the Mells Estate since the Reformation – and his brother-in-law, Raymond Asquith, the son of the wartime Prime Minister H.H. Asquith (1852–1928). All here, on this memorial at least, are equal.

Of course, Edward and Raymond further memorialised in the church. Though in life Edward had been a caricature of the bumbling, conceited and irresponsible landed gentry, he was also loyal, charming and found purpose and courage in the war. In November 1917, he took a bullet to the stomach in France and died at the age of 28. His bronze memorial by Sir Alfred Munnings (1878–1959) dominates the church interior.

Raymond, who was married to Frances' daughter Katherine, also died in France aged 37. He is remembered, in eleven lines of Latin cut into the stone of the church walls. A bronze wreath of olive branches is

placed above. Below, two hooks are fixed where his sword once rested – since removed for safekeeping. This is the warrior soldier of the Great War remembered. An attempt to rescue some triumph and gallantry from the wreckage of an awful, bloody war.

Aptly, the war poet Siegfried Sassoon (1886–1967) is buried in the churchyard.

Temple Church, City of London Greater London

In around 1119, a French knight, Hugues de Payens, led the creation of a military order, to protect Christian pilgrims on the routes to Jerusalem. Known as the Poor Soldiers of Christ and the Temple of Solomon (where they were headquartered), they came to be known as the Knights Templar.

Soon funds were being raised across Europe to bolster the Knights Templar and their work in protecting the flow of pilgrims on their way to the Holy Land. By the mid-twelfth century, the order was in need of a grand HQ for their London chapter. In 1185, Temple Church was completed and consecrated by the Patriarch of Jerusalem. Tucked away from the nearby bustle of the Strand, down Temple Lane, this is where the Knights Templar would have lived, prayed and worked until their dissolution in the early fourteenth century.

Modelled after the Anastasis Rotunda of the Church of the Holy Sepulchre in Jerusalem, it was a recreation of the holiest of Christian pilgrimage sites on English soil.

Jerusalem was builded here. On the floor of the church, nine effigies of some of the Templar Knights still can be seen laying there as if guarding the buildings, complete with swords and armour. These include William Marshal (c.1146/7–1219), Earl of Pembroke and the great knight who served five English kings, and is credited as playing a decisive role in the issuing of Magna Carta. You can still visit Temple Church and think back to these knights being initiated into the order, candlelight flickering over the elegant early Gothic architecture, over religious paintings, and through the monastic chants.

The carved Norman west doorway would once have ushered visitors into this sacred interior. Plans are afoot to once more make it the threshold through which pilgrims enter the building. Originally the church would have only had a small chancel. This was replaced in the middle of the thirteenth century with the elegant Gothic work which, while heavily restored, still captures the spirit and drama of the medieval past.

The Connoisseur

Searching for Treasures Within English Churches

As the years went by and I stumbled ever deeper into the labyrinth of English parish churches, certain treasures would call to me from the pages of dusty old guides or the screens of fellow social media wanderers. Those rare fifteenth-century font covers – pinnacles, crockets and finials reaching for eternity above; shimmering glass where beasts and saints alike have modulated the rise and fall of the sun for centuries; medieval screens so elegant and intricately carved as to give rise to a physical yearning to see them in person. So it was that I often found myself travelling up and down the country, whenever I had a spare day or two, in search of these missing treasures. I say missing, as in some way I conceived of these items as ones I needed to somehow collect, to visually stamp into my personal gallery of the beautiful and the curious.

The Church of the Holy Trinity, Blythburgh Suffolk

I'd seen the Blythburgh angel roof in so many photos and still wasn't prepared for its true magnificence. Passing through the south porch, I creaked open the big fifteenth-century wooden door, surprised by a rush of space and light that I hadn't expected. A handsome spread of red bricks and clay tile flooring led the way beyond the slim high pillars of the south arcade and out into a massive nave, the light doubled for the large clerestory windows above. My eyes lifted into the roof timbers where they met almost human faces, elegant and authoritative, wings spread proud and wide behind them, hands clutching shields in slender fingers. Although fixed in pairs each angel has their own distinct character and decorative scheme. To the medieval mind, these characters were real, beseeched to guide them through the tribulations of life, to be by their side, guardians against temptation and spiritual peril. Those parishioners would have laboured in the marshy flats of Suffolk and come in here to worship under their heavenly protectors. Much of the original paintwork is still visible, a faded indication of the kaleidoscope of late medieval devotional art.

Once there were around 20 angels. Decay and destruction have taken several, but those which survive still bear the arms of the families who rebuilt this church in the first half of the fifteenth century. The woodcarvers they commissioned must have been among the most accomplished available. What struck me about this roof above all else was the delicacy of the angels. They are watchful, stately, somehow maintaining their celestial aura and sovereignty. Put simply, they aren't just fantastic pieces of social and religious history. They are beautiful and valuable artworks in their own right. No wonder Blythburgh is often mentioned when church connoisseurs discuss their favourites.

To be entirely fair to Holy Trinity, it has much else to offer. Of particular note are the carved bench ends, associated folk tales, and the building's stupendous architectural coherence. It really is among the first rank of English parish churches. Before leaving, I climbed the little winding stairs up to a low prayer room above the porch: a hidden place, sequestered from the world and its troubles.

St Mary of the Assumption, Ufford Suffolk

William Dowsing (1596–1668) entered this church one afternoon in August 1644. He was a government official charged with overseeing that the works that needed to be done had been done. Those works were the removal of idolatrous images. His full title was 'Commissioner for the Destruction of Monuments of Idolatry and Superstition'. This was state-sanctioned iconoclasm. Old 'Smasher Dowsing' gets blamed for a lot. Then again, he made the mistake of recording his industry in a notorious diary of destruction. As such, he's known as the man who despoiled East Anglia's rich churches and his memory lingers on, infamous in the eastern counties. No doubt he thought he was doing God's work.

He'd already been to Ufford some eight months prior to that August visit. His aim then was to ensure a haul of images, glass and sculptures were removed.

Ufford, Jan. 27. We brake down 30 superstitious pictures; and gave direction to take down 37 more; and 4 cherubims to be takeing down of wood; and the chancel levelled

Why did he return? We can't quite be sure. He was checking up on something. It seems the churchwardens delayed him a few hours. Perhaps a tactic to get rid of him, tired of his nitpicking and thinking their job was done. Eventually Dowsing got in. He noted the 'glorious' telescopic font cover. 'Like a pope's triple crown', he scoffed. But it remained. The idolatrous sculptural works in its niches would have already been gone and perhaps Dowsing didn't think it was worth the effort to get these tiresome people to remove the cover as well. Who knows. Is it possible he acquiesced in the face of its beauty, bending his religious fervour to self-evident charm? We can only speculate. I suspect he just couldn't be bothered.

Rising 18 ft, in telescopic tiers of crockets and pinnacles, I watched this masterpiece of intricate woodwork pierce the morning sun as it blended through shafts of heavy incense at this Anglo-Catholic Church. Topped by a Pelican of Piety, representing Christ's self-sacrifice and with long faded but original paintwork, it was a wondrous sight to behold. I've seen other similar covers, but Ufford has to be the most glorious. I could well imagine these objects evolving parish by parish into incrementally more elaborate forms as late medieval English religion reached its crescendo of fervour. Motivated by the devotion of wealthy donors, it wouldn't be a surprise if local pride and one-upmanship played a role in such fantastical near bonkers manifestations of sacramental teaching.

St John the Baptist, Plymtree Devon

A gale was blowing as I approached St John's, trees swaying wildly in the churchyard. I love being in historic churches when it's howling outside. Listening to the creak of ancient timbers, feeling protected and safe. These buildings have known many a storm.

Inside, I was met by the vicar and two accomplices. I'm not sure what their roles were. Organ player? Churchwarden? I couldn't be sure. In a few weeks a local couple were getting married and they were coming in that morning for the customary pre-match chat. While these parish grandees waited for the couple, it was their pleasure to show me the screen they were so proud of. Even in a county famed for its old screens, this was among the very best, they were sure to tell me.

The screen has no less than 34 figures painted on it, probably dating from the late fifteenth century. My tour guides pointed out most of these. There was St Anthony the hermit. *'Can you see the pig at his feet?'* The Adoration of the Magi spread across four panels – I was told about some errant story of the three kings being contemporary royal and clergy, *'for which there is no evidence whatsoever!'*

St James the Great prompted me to tell them about my aborted pilgrimage to the Santiago de Compostela in Spain, along the Way of St James. My personal favourite was a sad character holding their own head with a scythe resting across them. I'd forgotten who I was told this was when looking at my photos afterwards. Thankfully, the author and medievalist Amy Jeffs was able to help me out. 'Sidwell!' she messaged back.

The much-venerated Sidwell, or Sidwella, gave rise to a cult in Devon and specifically in the cathedral city of Exeter. Sidwell's stepmother, jealous of her youth and inheritance, was said to have hired a corn reaper to scythe off her head. This seems a bit harsh but there is a silver lining. On the spot where the head came to rest a spring bubbled up and the Holy Well of St Sidwell was born, venerated by pilgrims for centuries to come. Many of the saints at Plymtree show signs of iconoclasm. Well, some of their eyes have been gouged out.

These paintings alone are worth a detour, but it's the top of the screen that makes Plymtree particularly special. Here the fan vaulting and four rows of carved floral decoration above are rich, lavish and arresting. They demand attention. I suspect the screen may have been repainted and gilded at some point, though everything has mellowed now to pleasing effect.

St Helen, Ranworth Norfolk

I visited St Helen's as a child. I've a vivid memory of dawdling behind my parents, kicking the grass, as we followed my mum to yet another church. Looking back, those 90s' boating holidays on the Norfolk Broads are some of my fondest memories. It seemed a hopeful time.

I returned to Ranworth some 20 years later, on the day Donald Trump was confirmed as the 45th President of the United States. It was grey and raining, and I and a close friend were on a mini-break. He'd asked to come church exploring with me. To get away from the pressures of his job for a few days. So, into East Anglia we went. The Broads and Ranworth were the answer.

The late fifteenth-century rood screen at Ranworth is the best I've seen. In the central lower panels are the twelve apostles carrying their emblems and dressed in fine garments. Above are open arches leading to fans of gilded ribs. Floral decorations of red, green and gold are painted onto a white background. These were painstakingly cleaned in the 1960s. What a job that must have been – to remove centuries of grime, delicate touch by delicate touch, and see those gorgeous colours emerge.

To the left is a chapel dedicated to St John the Baptist. Most notable on this side of the screen is the projecting wing on which St George appears in his armour of white with a red cross, stamping on the dragon under his feet, sword held high and proud. Across from good old St George is the no less triumphant St Michael, who, as commander of the Army of God, goes further, slaying a seven-headed dragon. It's stirring stuff.

Thankfully the testosterone is brought under control in the Lady Chapel to the right. St Mary Salome, The Virgin Mary, St Mary Cleophas and St Margaret of Antioch are arranged above an altar. It was a humbling experience to sit on a nearby pew and work from my guidebook to the paintings and back again. St Margaret of Antioch was patron saint of childbirth and it was here that women would come to kneel in prayer, asking for protection during the anguished period of their term. These saints had suffered on Earth and, as such, were sympathetic to human pain and fragility. Social history like this in English churches is of national importance.

After admiring the rood screen, we worked our way up to the top of the tower. It's a rare treat to be able to do this. Here we looked over Ranworth Broad and the surrounding nature reserve. I think my friend felt a lot better for it, even on such a miserable day.

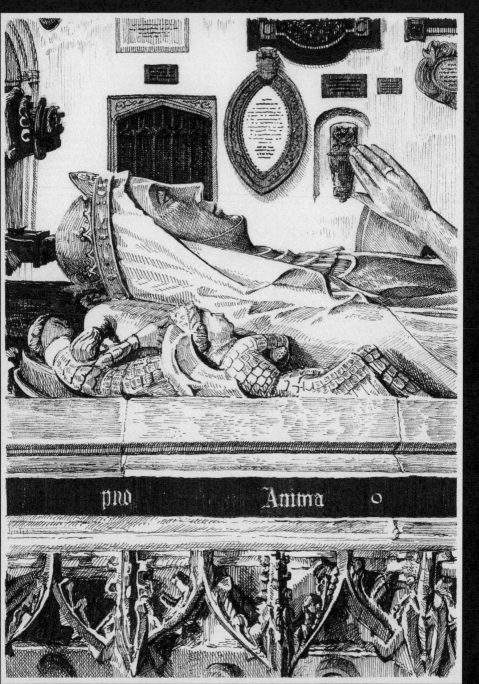

St Mary the Virgin, Ewelme Oxfordshire

When I first travelled to Ewelme the church was locked. At the parsonage they told me I'd been particularly unlucky – conservation work was taking place that week and the interior couldn't be accessed. These are the hard and heavy tribulations of the avid church crawler. Within that opulent fifteenth-century church was the chest tomb of Alice de la Pole (c.1404–75), one of the finest late Gothic funerary monuments in the country. I would return.

Alice was the granddaughter of Geoffrey Chaucer (c.1340–1400), author of *The Canterbury Tales*. By just 24, she'd been widowed twice. These were uncertain and fragile times. Woe befell Alice's third husband too, William de la Pole (1396–1450), Duke of Suffolk. He rose to dominate the government of Henry VI in the 1440s, having negotiated the king's marriage to Margaret of Anjou (1430–82) as part of peace efforts to conclude the Hundred Years' War with France. As it was, William would go on to take the blame for England's defeats in the later stages of that epic inter-generational conflict. Banished from the kingdom for five years, William was intercepted in the channel and beheaded – a gruesome expression of the discontent surrounding his influence on the king as well as the perceived weakness of the Lancastrian dynasty. Alice wouldn't marry again and in

time switched allegiances to the House of York, even becoming custodian of the queen she once served, Margaret of Anjou.

Between the chancel and the chapel of St John the Baptist, Alice's alabaster effigy lies dignified atop an imposing tomb. The Order of the Garter on her left arm, a flight of gold flecked angels fluffing up her pillow, hands clasped in prayer as they have been for near 550 years. On the sides of the chest are more angels, neatly arranged and bearing family shields. Hidden below all this is an intricately carved grill through which the shadowy cadaver of Alice can be seen, a humble *memento mori* to balance the grandeur and luxury on display elsewhere. Every touch of high-Gothic spectacle has been ranged for the awesome task of memorialising Alice's life, to keep her in the prayers of the living. Three times I left the chapel only to return, to take one last look at the carved memory of this extraordinary woman.

St Mary the Virgin, Sparham Norfolk

Against the north aisle of this tucked away Norfolk church is propped a macabre *memento mori* – a reminder of our inevitable fate. The church was built in the fourteenth and fifteenth centuries. A flint tower rises above a wild church. On a peaceful country lane it provides the near perfect setting for the Gothic masterpiece inside. I entered to find the interior cool, stiff, almost stagnant. Making my way through the nave arcades, I could see what I had come for. It's hard to avert the gaze from the sudden intensity and power of late medieval religious art such as this. These works were designed to shock, to urge parishioners to consider the transience of life, to prepare for death while there was time.

Knees on the flagstones, the late fifteenth-century Sparaham corpse panels were before me. In the first panel, two dandyish cadavers parade their finery. To the right, a female skeleton wears a dress embellished by polka dot sleeves and lapels, a tight black belt decorated by golden flowerheads, the same as her necklace. In her hands she holds a posy of flowers, proffering them to the male figure on the left. Taken from *The Book of Job*, the Latin has been translated as: '*Man that is born of woman hath but a few days and is full of trouble. He comes forth like a flower and is cut down.*'

The gentleman is arguably even more ghastly. A black feather in his cap, a gold chain and green cape, his spine, ribs and skeletal fingers are on display. The couple reminded me of the charming, learned, cane-wielding depiction of Satan in Mikhail Bulgakov's satire of the Stalinist state, *The Master and Margarita*. There is visual entertainment here, all the better to draw the viewer in.

On the second panel, to the left, a shrouded skeleton points to a font and the Latin reads: '*I should have been as though I had not been born, I should have been carried from the womb to the grave.*' This is also taken from *The Book of Job* and may be interpreted as Job's fixation and despair at life's tribulations and the darkness of death. It might seem a gloomy note to include in a parish church, where it would have once formed the dado of the rood screen. In the wider context of the redemptive message of Christ, its message is transformed. When eternal salvation awaits the pious, to focus on the trivial vanities and pleasures of the world would be a dreadful mistake.

Further on is a panel featuring St Walstan (*c.*975–1016), with scythe, and St Thomas of Canterbury (*c.*1118–70). Painted in gold, green and red the panel surround is delightfully decorated. In another church this would be a knockout. However, at Sparham, the corpse panels are what you really need to see.

St Peter & St Paul, Chaldon Surrey

St Peter & St Paul's sits in the first breath of countryside to wrestle itself from the clutches of London. I arrived over the chalk and grasslands of Farthing Downs before taking the old lane down to Chaldon.

This church is distinct for its remarkable 17 ft-wide mural, painted around 1200, in a style quite unlike any other church wall painting in England. Depicted is the ladder of salvation rising up from purgatory in a striking burnt ochre and cream composition. As with many of these paintings, the Chaldon mural was discovered beneath the whitewashed west wall in the nineteenth century – in this case, around 1870. It dominates the visitor as soon as they enter the nave, vying for attention against the chancel opposite in this small country church. Some have speculated the artist was a peripatetic monk taking influences from as far away as Greece. The truth is no one knows who painted this remarkable piece, or where they drew their inspiration. It's a unique work of tremendous imagination and creativity, which for me is explanation enough.

Vivid. Vital. Elemental.

The centrepiece of the painting is the ladder which cuts the painting vertically into four quadrants. Naked souls struggle to climb the ladder towards heaven where Christ appears in a cloud. Some are successful, others tumble into the abyss. At the bottom of the painting, devils punish the seven deadly sins.

These are inventively portrayed, some easier to interpret than others. Avarice is probably the most obvious. In the lower right-hand side of the painting a man is forced to squat over a fire, three bags of coins weighing him down and more pouring from his mouth. It's a fun game to try and find all the sins. Some are probably impossible without the guidebook. The artist also sought to emphasise the hopelessness of these hellish conditions. On a spiked beam held up by two larger devils, souls are put to work. Futility reigns. A blacksmith presses on without an anvil, a potter without a wheel. The toil of mortal life continues, stripped of purpose and output.

The upper half of the painting is less gloomy and arguably even more bizarre. In the upper-right quadrant, Satan appears to have been vanquished as he lies prostrate on a giant worm like creature, the flames of hell rising in the background, his head being pierced by its beak. Christ stands triumphant above, holding his right hand to a line of souls whose arms are outstretched in supplication. In the upper-left quadrant, St Michael weighs souls, while a devil tries to tilt the scales in his favour – a common and recurring image utilised in similar Doom paintings for centuries to come.

There are countless other observations to be made here at the Chaldon wall painting. I was eased away by the offer of tea and cake by the vicar. We chatted away with some of the parishioners. She was highly concerned about the climate crisis and had been to a number of protests. They'd made the churchyard wildlife friendly. How lovely my pilgrimage to Chaldon was.

St Peter, Wenhaston Suffolk

The story of the Wenhaston Doom painting is truly astonishing. In 1892, the east end of the church was being renovated and the old whitewashed boards wedged behind a royal coat of arms were pulled out plank by plank and put into the churchyard. Overnight it rained and the wash on those panels began to dissolve. When workmen went back to dispose of this waste timber, they were staring down at the Virgin Mary and John the Baptist. Painted in the early sixteenth century to convey the message of the Last Judgement, these panels would have formed the backdrop for the rood cross above the chancel arch. How thankful we can be for that downpour. The panels were rescued, reassembled, and are now displayed in the north aisle.

It's rare to be able to get so close to a Doom painting. In fact, it's relatively rare to see one at all. At St Peter's you are able to negotiate the tables and chairs of parish coffee mornings and nose about this fascinating creation at eye level. Unlike other examples I've seen, the Wenhaston Doom has been split into a variety of scenes so as to make space for a rood and two attendant sculptural figures, almost certainly Mary and John. Long since removed, only the empty outline of these lost elements is now left as blank wood.

My eyes were immediately drawn to the monsters and demons on the bottom right of the Doom. St Michael weighs a soul against a pair of demons as the Devil pleads with him for it. Next are the damned, chained by a team of demons and forced into the terrifying mouth of hell, depicted literally as a gigantic, fanged beast. Elsewhere is some hope for the penitent viewer. Christ in Majesty is perched on a rainbow at the top of the Doom. The Virgin Mary and John the Baptist kneel towards him in prayer, the dead rising from their graves in the background. On the bottom left, St Peter holds the keys of heaven as he talks to a naked group of souls. They haven't been saved yet, though further to the left some fortunate souls can be seen being greeted in what appears to be the castle-like palace of heaven.

St Michael, Castle Frome Herefordshire

You only really come to St Michael's to see the colossal font. Carved from a single piece of stone at the end of the twelfth century, the bowl displays the four Evangelists in the form of the 'living creatures' that surround God's throne (Rev 4:7) – the angel for St Matthew, the lion for St Mark, the winged ox for St Luke, and the eagle for St John. Also featured is the Baptism of Christ in the Jordan River where the hand and spirit of God descend on Jesus. By his feet are four little fish, crisply carved in a concentric ring of watery ripples. Beneath is the plinth where the weight of the font presses down on three figures – only one sad-looking figure survives intact. The suggestion in the guidebook is that the act of baptism is casting off the evil and sin represented by these figures. Others have cast doubt on this theory. Whatever the case, this is one of the most important and finely executed Norman carvings in England.

The font is bundled into the Herefordshire School of Romanesque sculptural works. The interlaced decoration on the font in all its twists and turns displays the great skill of the carvers. Scholars have identified inspiration for this work as being drawn from Italy and Spain. However, when infused with the Viking and Celtic influences of the Herefordshire School, this piece of sculptural art should be seen as part of a solidly English outpouring of artistic expression.

What will never cease to amaze me is where these great pieces can be found. If this font were placed in one of the big London museums, it would punch admirably for attention by virtue of its beauty and national importance. I'm glad it's not. I'm glad it's here. In situ, in Herefordshire where it has been for hundreds of years. Still, we shouldn't be fooled by the circumstances in which we find this font. It remains one of England's masterpieces.

St Edward, Stow-on-the-Wold Gloucestershire

The legendary north porch of St Edward's is lined by a pair of veteran yew trees said to be J. R. R. Tolkein's (1892–1973) inspiration for the

Doors of Durin, the west gate of Moria, in *The Lord of the Rings*. It's a claim never verified though he was known to have travelled the area extensively during his long career as the Rawlinson and Bosworth Professor of Anglo-Saxon at Oxford University. Whether this connection is true or coincidental, something of the Cotswolds is forever present in Tolkein's Shire. He cherished this countryside and knew how precious it truly is.

St Edward's sits behind the square of the quintessential Cotswold market town: Stow-on-the-Wold. Visitors come see the famous Tolkein door and take in the bucolic surroundings of chocolate-box England. It wasn't always so calm. In the churchyard is a memorial to the Battle of Stow, fought on 21 March 1646 – one of the final decisive open battles of the first English Civil War. Here Sir Jacob Astley (1579–1652) was intercepted while marching Royalist forces to meet King Charles I at Oxford. Detachments of the parliamentarian New Model Army encircled Astley, attacking via a series of pre-dawn raids in the darkened lanes of nearby villages. Retreating to Stow, defeat inevitable, the Royalists broke and fled. Some 1,500 men were imprisoned in the church, 200 more were slaughtered in the market square. The story is told that Astley surrendered with the words: '*Well, boys, you have done your work, now you may go and play – if you don't fall out among yourselves*.' Whenever I walk in the Cotswolds I think of those marauding bands of soldiers. England's soil has known much bloodletting.

Tolkien, too, had experienced the horrors of war, how a hellscape can emerge. In the summer of 1916, he joined the British Expeditionary Force on the Western Front. Serving as signalling officer in the 11th Battalion of the Lancashire Fusiliers, he was to be responsible for overseeing communications between the front line and their superiors – affording him a unique insight into what he would describe as the 'animal horror' of war.

The Somme offensive began on 1 July 1916. At 7 a.m., the whistles sounded and wave after wave of soldiers began to go over the top. Around 20,000 were shot dead in the open field, 35,000 wounded. The bloodiest day in the history of the British army. A few miles back from the front, Tolkein would survive that disastrous first day. In the coming months, he would witness further disasters, the battlefield reduced to a quagmire of thickening mud. It was trench fever that brought an end to his war. Tolkein was invalided back to England in November of that year, the campaign ending mid-November. The memories of that war would haunt him forever.

Inside the church is a notable incised memorial to an earlier warrior, the Royalist Captain Hastings Keyte (1621–46), who perished at the Battle of Stow-on-the-Wold. Two skulls sit below a proud image of Keyte, complete with flowing locks.

The Church of St Mary, Fairford Gloucestershire

To step inside St Mary's is to be caught in a great chamber of dazzling colour. It possesses the most complete collection of medieval glass remaining in any English parish church. In total 28 windows of narrative glass, relaying nothing less than the story of the Christian Church. From the Old Testament to the life of Christ, from the early Christian Church to the final judgement awaiting in the great west window. In fact, Fairford might just be the only parish church to have kept all of its original decorative glass in place, more or less – even here there has been some small damage and replacement.

Estimates vary, but roughly 8,000 pre-Reformation churches still stand in England. In terms of heritage value, Fairford, by means of the survival of its glass alone, represents one of the most important parish churches in England. The historian Alec Clifton-Taylor (1907–85) argued that, 'the wholesale destruction of medieval stained glass was the greatest calamity that has ever befallen English art'. It is therefore incalculably valuable to have this example of how many of our pre-Reformation churches would have been illuminated by the murmurs of dawn, the fires of the sun's zenith, the fall of twilight.

The glass at Fairford was fired over 500 years ago, at the beginning of the sixteenth century. It has been attributed to the Westminster workshop of Barnard Flower: the royal glazier. Nevertheless, some have argued the glass isn't quite the most accomplished – Fairford's notoriety more a reflection of the fact it exists rather than quality of the artistry on display. Perhaps there is an element of truth in this. Even so, we shouldn't be too harsh in our judgements.

Fairford has its moments and no short supply of intrigues and amusements. The depiction of the Last Judgement in the great west window is the best example. Christ on the customary rainbow above, St Michael in golden armour weighing souls below, and on the bottom right a deep-red and blue image of hell. Here a wild cast of beasts and demons gleefully torture the damned. It is a maniacal, tempestuous composition that caused me to think of the darkness and anguish of Francisco Goya's (1746–1828) 'Black Paintings'.

The formidable 'wool Gothic' churches still conduct the scenery over this most idyllic slice of English countryside. Fairford was built from the foundations in the 1490s. Cirencester wool merchant John Tame (c.1430–1500) was the money man in this instance. His family arms can still be seen on the tower. In 1520, King Henry VIII (1491–1547; r.1509–47) stayed in Fairford. It seems likely this pious king would have attended Mass in the Church – it was well before his break with the Catholic Church – under the freshly installed glass that remains in place to this day.

St Mary the Virgin, Higham Kent

'I'm going to the north Kent marshes to see a door,' I said to my flatmate while he recovered from a Friday night hangover. Higham was my destination at the base of the Hoo Peninsula. A few hours later, I pulled into a small station next to a commuter car park among a scattering of 1970s' housing. In the rising heat, I slowly ascended a hill a mile or so up to the outlying church sealed by my coveted door. Agricultural and industrial debris floated about in the breeze, a golden haze over cracked earth and crumbling tarmac. It's exceedingly difficult to describe how mesmerising and odd this place is. It's disconcerting, eerie, brooding; a haunted landscape where the wastes of man mingle with a marshy brilliance.

In 1856, writer Charles Dickens (1812–70) bought a country retreat in Higham. Soon he would take the surrounding landscape and make it echo through the generations. 'Ours was the marsh country' announces the opening page of *Great Expectations*, drawing us into the isolated world of Philip Pirrip. Caring for churches in both Higham and nearby Cooling, the Churches Conservation Trust advertises a walk between these two buildings as a 'Dickensian stroll in the North Kent Marshes'. I'm not sure what I'd expected of this. Countryside, I suppose. Nature. Calm. I got something quite different.

First, I was to explore St Mary's. The church once sat next to a nunnery. By the start of the sixteenth century, only five nuns remained, two pregnant by the local priest. The institution was dissolved soon after, more than a decade before the suppression of religious houses began in earnest.

Charmingly carved, the weighty south door I'd come to see is late-fourteenth or early fifteenth century and decorated by traceried panels with regularly positioned flowerheads and a few human faces. A Green Man-type figure is placed on the left-hand side. At the apex is a bird. I made this out to be a 'Pelican in Piety'. In medieval bestiaries, the Pelican pecked at its breast to help revive its offspring – an allusion to the blood Christ gave to save humankind. Higham's notable wooden pulpit might have been carved at the same time. There is also a dark and heavy wooden fifteenth-century screen.

Dickens' daughter, Kate, married here in July 1860. However, it wasn't St Mary's that directly sparked his imagination. That honour falls to St James' at Cooling.

I eventually made it to the second church of the day. It's here that the opening scenes of *Great Expectations* play out. Where the tragic graves of 13 infants helped Dickens conceive of an orphan contemplating his lost family and the 'dark flat wilderness beyond the churchyard, intersected with dykes and mounds and gates'.

Journeys of Contemplation

Calm in a Chaotic World

I always know the old churches of England will be waiting
for me to return. Familiar friends and those I'm yet to meet.
They provide their solace and sanctuary without judgement
or condition, 'come, sit for a time and know there have been
many here before'. I tread the footpaths to these churches in
all weathers of emotion. Sometimes, I know I must go. When I
least have the energy to do so, when overwhelmed by the world,
lost in its roar. Off I go to some little train station, some tangled
country lane, and make my way to commune with the old
stones, to run my hand over smooth worn wood, to better know
the human hopes and grief blotted into these places. Somehow,
I always feel a little better for it.

St Peter, Wiggenhall St Peter Norfolk

I left the train at Watlington and walked down Station Road to the gloomy leveed banks of the River Great Ouse. Once part of a vast storm absorbing wild stretching across some 1,500 square miles of Cambridgeshire, Norfolk and Lincolnshire, this part of the country is known as 'the Fens'. The uncluttered hush, the enshrouding mists, have for centuries, perhaps millennia, given way to a colourful cast of folk Fenland characters. This is the land of the bog spirit Tiddy Mun; where ghostly lantern men stalked the horizon; where flickering will-o'-the-wisps lured unsuspecting travellers into their watery fastness; revered cunning folk healed ailments and warded off evil spirits. It is a place I love to visit.

Today, the fields have been drained and the rivers long since hemmed in, contained. Still, the memories of those isolated pre-drainage marshland communities live on. Above that muddy, thick river and buffeted by marshland winds, I could see the open bones of St Peter's before me. Red brick and stone, this church is now a romantic roofless ruin having fallen into disrepair in the first half of the twentieth century. Thankfully, the decline has now been halted and the ivy slashed back, leaving a largely fifteenth-century structure to be explored. I stopped in the nave and faced the wide moody sky of East Anglia. There's something disconcerting about such a place being so recently ruined, a reminder that all things will pass eventually.

After St Peter's, I pushed onwards into this land of churches. Sky, earth, water and megaliths of faith – what I was to later term the 'Wiggenhall Loop' – must be one of the best historic church walks in England. Still to be explored were Wiggenhall St Germans, Wiggenhall St Mary the Virgin and, at the end of the walk, as the light faded, Wiggenhall St Mary Magdalen. Here, I grabbed my dinner from the little chippy on the corner of a suburban cul-de-sac and made my way back to the station.

As the train pulled out on its way back to London and a spit of rain hit the darkened windows, I felt almost relieved to be leaving the disconcerting clutches of marshland. Of course, I knew I'd be back. There is a wild and compelling underbelly to the seeming monotony of the Fens.

St John the Baptist, Sutterby Lincolnshire

I was greeted by the farmer and sensed that someone came by every couple of months or so to take a look at St John the Baptist's. Coming here is to glimpse how isolated life must have been centuries ago. That sense of isolation gathers as you walk up the overgrown footpath to the church itself, a small building barely identifiable as a church at all. Sutterby is an out-of-the-way place. Yet a calmness accompanies it, as if a test asking you to be still and with yourself for a time.

The church is of Norman origins. An incredibly rugged and narrow Norman doorway can be seen if you squash down the undergrowth on the north side of the building. Elsewhere, much has changed in the subsequent eight centuries or so, as is most often the case. The font is fourteenth century and a nineteenth-century screen integrates fragments of medieval tracery. Some traces of wall paintings can be seen too, perhaps one being the Royal Arms of Charles II (1630–1685; r.1660–85). It's not for the historic details that you come to Sutterby though. It's a place for quiet and solitude. In the tiny nave were two cord chairs. I sat

on one of them and listened to the shifting breeze and birdsong outside.

Sutterby is a Scandinavian place name – 'the settlement of the shoemaker' – always small, it was further depopulated in the wake of the Black Death. Remarkably, it struggled on as a parish church until 1935. Since 1981, it's been in the care of the wonderfully named Friends of Friendless Churches. I'm profoundly grateful such friends exist. The moments of peace these buildings provide are invaluable.

All Saints, Saltfleetby Lincolnshire

Lincolnshire is a big county full of out-of-the-way tumbledown churches. The geographic isolation, the relatively low population density, and a lack of industry have conspired to leave them untouched and astonishing. Few places would I more readily recommend for the connoisseur of atmospheric old English churches than Lincolnshire.

And of these Lincolnshire churches there are few better paragons of age and abandonment than Saltfleetby. Almost every century of England's history is written into the fabric of this building. The simple 'Y' tracery windows looking out from the nave are probably *c.*1300. The leaning tower, heavily buttressed against its westward yearning, has upper sections from the fifteenth century, while the base is thirteenth century.

This seemingly forgotten church has one of the most compelling interiors I have ever visited. How the ages weep here. Rich layers of medieval community, of faith in the storms of life out on the fringe of our island. Only the groans of the blustery sea wind to keep me company.

The beautiful screens were listed as fourteenth century though to my relatively untrained eye looked a little later. There are two pulpits, one Elizabethan, one seventeenth century, donated from Oriel College, Oxford. Great church bells sat on the floor near a long silent pump organ. Someone clearly loves this place. There were flowers and pot plants dotted about on tables and the raised base of the font. Yet the modern chairs in the nave were sticky, as were the old hymn books. Perhaps there is a carol service here once a year. It would be nice to think so. The building is in the care of the Churches Conservation Trust. They need all the help they can get to help support such special buildings.

All Saints, Walesby Lincolnshire

As evening began to settle, I climbed the gentle sloping hillside up to the 'ramblers church', All Saints, high over the Lincolnshire Wolds. In the early twentieth century, another church was built in Walesby nearer the main residential streets. With the 'old church' being somewhat out of the way it unsurprisingly fell out of use and was left to moulder until being rescued in the 1930's.

The old church was soon taken up as a place of pilgrimage and rest by walkers, becoming particularly popular with those following the 'Viking Way' through Lincolnshire, Leicestershire and Rutland. So important was the building to this community that a stained-glass window depicting walkers and cyclists was donated by the Grimsby Wayfarers Association in 1951. How aged and rugged the interior looked as I stood before that window, a little makeshift altar put up below it with a single pot jug and a plastic sheet, likely in place to protect from the bat droppings. The nave arcades looked endearingly simple to me, semi-circular and likely late twelfth century. Some sort of move towards 'stiff leaf' carving on the capitals had been made, an early indication of the transition toward Early English Gothic. A quite fine Jacobean pulpit stands next to the chancel arch.

It is from the exterior that Walesby really begins to sing. Honeyed ironstone on its escarpment set against lush green English countryside. Little could be better. I sat on a nearby bench and made some notes before it got too dark and I knew I had to be on my way. Finally, I'd paid my respects to the old ramblers' church of Walesby.

St Cuthbert, Bewcastle Cumbria

I made it to Bewcastle in the early morning after negotiating the moors of this most northerly extreme of England. Hadrian's Wall lies some seven miles to the south. It is remote country. Once there was a Roman Fort at Bewcastle, a scouting outpost in use from the mid-second century until the frontier watch was disbanded in the decades before the Roman withdrawal from Britain. St Cuthbert's sits within the banked remnants of the fort. It was impossible not to think of those men who would have once stared into open country from this, the edge of the Roman Empire. Archaeological evidence suggests the auxiliary unit who manned Bewcastle were drawn from Dacia, in modern-day eastern Romania. How they must have cursed those feral snow-heaped winters.

I'd come here to see an object that appeared long after the Romans left the fort to ruin and decay: the Bewcastle Cross. The cross is thought to date from the eighth century, though possibly earlier. Undoubtedly, it is one of the finest surviving Anglo-Saxon artworks in the country and sits proudly south of the church where it has defied the elements for some 1,300 years or more. Runic inscriptions can still be made out. So far, they seem to have evaded full interpretation. Figurative interlacing adds to the decoration and elsewhere is the figure of Jesus, his feet resting on the snouts of animal-like creatures. Each morning the sun shines on the east of the cross, where scrollwork references the Tree of Life. Scholars have suggested the cross imports a visual language familiar to those lay members of the community while imbuing these naturalistic images with fresh biblical meaning - to absorb latent instincts within the framework of the new religion.

To explore Bewcastle in the crisp early morning light was a deep pleasure. The legendary architectural historian Nicolaus Pevsner (1902–83) once described Bewcastle (along with another similar cross in Ruthwell, Dumfriesshire) as 'the greatest achievement of their date in the whole of Europe'.

I left the churchyard thinking of the vast swirl of humanity that had touched this spot down the centuries. The rise and fall of civilisations, new faiths kindled and artworks transmitted across continents. There was a contentment to be found in all this. A comfort in vast histories into which we enter and are wrapped in, consciously or not.

St Ninian, Brougham Cumbria

Known locally as Ninekirks, St Ninian's stands down a long track sweeping above the River Eamont, the Lake District rising up in the distance. It can only be visited on foot.

I'd long wanted to visit Ninekirks, having spied it on the map. There is something cathartic for me, as I have said, about the act of pilgrimage, be the distance small or long. For me, it is about the intention of setting out on a journey, putting aside the time for reflection and calm. Discovery always awaits, internal and external. This pilgrimage only took a few hours. At other times, I have walked hundreds of miles for weeks at a time. I always think of these journeys as pilgrimages though, for me it is the intention not the temporal duration that matters.

This church at Brougham sits nestled in its fields, surrounded by wildflowers and a grove of trees. Originally there was a Norman church on the site, but this version was rebuilt by Lady Anne Clifford in 1659. She wrote in her diary, '... and this Church of Nine Kirke would in all likelihood have fallen downe it was soe ruinous, if it had not been repayred by mee'.

The church is an unusual shape, flat and low in pinkish sandstone. The interior is gloomy and atmospheric, the structure of the building giving no room for large windows. Beyond the setting it is the original seventeenth-century, finely crafted woodwork that is worth seeing. Box pews and a three-decker pulpit dominate the interior, untouched since they were first installed.

The Churches Conservation Trust are now guardians of Ninekirks. They suggest listening to one of their 'mindful moments' at this church; 'a guided meditation to provide a moment of mindfulness, connection and reflection, peace and calm in hectic times'. I can see why.

I sat with my back against the old dry-stone wall of the churchyard, ate some sandwiches and a packet of crisps, and listened to the sounds of nature.

St Cyriac, Lacock Wiltshire

As one of England's best preserved medieval villages an array of films and TV shows have been filmed in Lacock, including *Pride and Prejudice*, *Downton Abbey* and, most famously, perhaps, the Harry Potter series. Alongside the abbey and wider estate, the village was gifted to the National Trust in 1944 by Matilda Talbot (1871–1958), niece of Henry Fox Talbot (1800–77), the famous photography pioneer. The visitors come here in their thousands and it is easy to see why.

First there is the abbey, a former Augustinian nunnery which came into the possession of the Sharington family in 1540, following Henry VIII's Dissolution of the Monasteries. The abbey church was demolished and the rest of the building converted into a family home. However, the glorious fifteenth-century cloisters survive, alive with the footsteps of the religious sisters who once paced up and down them. While the cloisters are a marvel and well-worth seeing, I imagine a lot of visitors miss out on the further architectural wonders held in nearby St Cyriac's, the parish church which stands a short walk away back in the village.

On my last visit here, I sat in the churchyard, taking in the chest tombs and watching the local parishioners file out from Sunday service beneath the octagonal spire added in the early seventeenth century. An elderly gentleman fixed his green woollen tie as he stepped out of the porch. A lady kindly told us, 'the church is open if you want to take a look. You're very welcome.' A little pride and infinite warmth in her voice. 'Thank you, that's very kind', I replied.

I always head straight to the polychrome Lady Chapel of *c*.1430. This is one of the most intricately carved and atmospheric spaces in the land. Standing below the pendant vaulting with its faded medieval paintwork is as close as I've felt to the intimate intensity of late-medieval worship. This chapel is also home to the Renaissance tomb of Sir William Sharington (*c*.1495–1553). Three carved panels on the front display the Sharington crest and a scorpion. It was William Sharington who first acquired Lacock Abbey from the Crown. It's a small space but I'm always drawn back to that corner of this church. The ages whisper on.

The main cruciform structure of the church came a little after the Lady Chapel in the middle of the fifteenth century. As such, when walking into the church you are met by a classic example of the Perpendicular-Gothic style, the high nave arcades bringing space and light. The chancel was completely rebuilt in the first years of the twentieth century, but this has been so sympathetically done it hardly seems noticeable at first glance.

The Final Word

Any concluding remarks to a book like this should really look to the future. What's next for England's church buildings when, by 2050, it's likely that regular attendance of Anglican churches will be really quite exceptional. A century before, it would have been commonplace, part of community life. But we have changed. What then for the church buildings that have sustained so much of our ritual life for centuries?

On this subject I will have to disappoint, at least to an extent. Giving any coherent answer seems quite frankly impossible. We can imagine the answers will come variously. Some precious artefacts and places will be tragically lost or diminished through decay and damage. Some churches will even fall into the sea, accelerated by the climatic changes we are to endure – such as the monumental late medieval church of St Mary's on the crumbling north Norfolk coastline at Happisburgh. The haphazard, slightly disorganised community feel to these places may become ever dustier laments to a bygone world, the sticky hymn books covered in cobwebs and droppings, as I have already seen more than once. Elsewhere, creativity and courage will secure the future of some of these buildings due to the efforts of dedicated local volunteers. New uses will be found to sit comfortably alongside the old ways, dutifully enjoyed at Easter and Christmas. The wonderful conservation bodies will play an ever-greater role, where they can secure funding. The Church of England will continue its long dialogue on the institution's responsibilities to these places. It will be messy and uneven yet the labyrinth of England's churches will struggle on, somehow, in some form.

If I were to offer some thoughts into this debate, I would give three:

First, these buildings are a spiritual inheritance, whether we come to them with faith or not. Previous generations poured their creativity, determination and love into the fabric of them. As such, they are imbued with the emotions of centuries of faith and community life. We would do well to remember how central they are to our story. It would, therefore, be a shame to entirely lose their unique atmosphere, the soothing pale light filtering over hushed stone, the quietude and solace they provide. Yet, whatever we do with these church buildings, their role as spiritual and community spaces should somehow be respected. Not out of some staid conservative impulse closed to change but to be embraced as an opportunity to reimagine, where necessary, what has been, while making the best of what we've inherited and will pass on.

Second, I renamed my Instagram account @englishpilgrim as I began increasingly to envision my visits to churches as mini pilgrimages, moments away from the swirl of life and a chance to contemplate. I have since undertaken some longer pilgrimages, most notably on the Camino de Santiago, the way across the north of Spain that ultimately leads to the tomb of St James in the Cathedral of Santiago de Compostela.

Pilgrimage seems to be having a revival at the moment. Our desire to find meaning or calm through contemplative walking remains. Do our churches have some role in this trend? I firmly believe the UK has a tremendous opportunity to build on its reputation as a pilgrimage destination. Our countryside and footpaths are wondrous assets. Our little towns and villages are full of creativity and small businesses ready to serve eager pilgrims. As rest stops, and even as accommodation, can our churches – ones such as those I have highlighted in this volume – help invigorate pilgrimage? As focal points on pilgrim routes they could be notable attractions, whether they be on ancient Christian pilgrim ways or modern secular reimaginings of what pilgrimage can be. Perhaps it is idealistic to think so, yet I've also been drawn to these ideals.

Third, any enlightened culture secretary of the UK government could do the nation an enduring service by improving the funding, organisation and

Watts Cemetery Chapel, Compton

recognition of the national collection that our church buildings represent. This should be a flagship cultural policy. If all the exhibits from our church buildings were gathered in one place, they would represent one of the most incredible museums ever gathered in all the world, in all its history. So often though, these exhibits sit unfunded, unconserved, in weatherbeaten corners of our parish churches. In a way, I like this. They are in situ, unbothered. And there is a deep romanticism in finding a fifteenth-century painting propped against some old box pew. But they provide England and Britain with so much historic and cultural value, that they need to be cared for accordingly. At the moment, everything feels a little chaotic.

I would like to see our parish churches considered as our most important national museums. Ones that aren't plastered with signage and gift shops but that are centrally funded, at least somewhat organised, the absolute gems of the collection properly and systematically cared for. A whole book could be written on this subject, but I just write these words in the faint hope they might find their way to someone, someday, who knows a culture secretary or someone in their team . . .

More than anything, I finish this book by encouraging everyone to get out and visit their historic church buildings. They are some of our premier cultural attractions and it shouldn't be unusual to visit a particular place for its church alone. If you cannot get out in person, then I hope you can at least enjoy vicariously the travels in this book, or those found on my social media accounts, as well as those of countless other enthusiasts. There are many of us. And, together, onwards we may go, further into the fascinating labyrinth of England's churches.

Index of Churches

Buckinghamshire
Jordans, Jordans Meeting House *123*

Cambridgeshire
Barnack, St John the Baptist *34*
Duxford, St John *102–5*

Cornwall
St Germans, St Germans Priory *45*
St Just in Roseland, St Just *97*
Trebetherick, St Enodoc *93*
Zennor, St Senara *95*

Cumbria
Bewcastle, St Cuthbert *165*
Brougham, St Ninian *167*

Derbyshire
Chelmorton, St John the Baptist *14*
Edensor, St Peter *13*
Eyam, St Lawrence *29*
Norbury, St Mary & St Barlock *14–17*
Tideswell, St John the Baptist *18*

Devon
Plymtree, St John the Baptist *134*

Dorset
Wimborne St Giles, St Giles *87*

East Sussex
Southease, St Peter *102*

Essex
Bradwell-on-Sea, St Peter-on-the-Wall *26*

Gloucestershire
Berkeley, St Mary the Virgin *68–70*
Duntisbourne Rouse, St Michael *90*
Fairford, St Mary *150*
Stow-on-the-Wold, St Edward *147–8*

Greater London
City of London, St Bartholomew the Great *100*
City of London, St Mary Woolnoth *83*
City of London, Temple Church *126*
Tower of London, St John's Chapel *39*
Westminster, St John *79–80*

Hampshire
Breamore, St Mary *30*
Winchester, Hospital of St Cross
   and Almshouse of Noble Poverty *42*

Herefordshire
Abbey Dore, Dore Abbey *46*
Castle Frome, St Michael *147*
Kilpeck, St Mary & St David *39–40*

Hertfordshire
Stanstead Abbotts, St James *83–4*

Kent
Canterbury, St Martin *25*
Higham, St Mary the Virgin *153*

Leicestershire
Stoke Golding, St Margaret of Antioch *59-60*

Lincolnshire
Heckington, St Andrew *63-4*
Saltfleetby, All Saints *160*
Sutterby, St John the Baptist *159*
Tattershall, Collegiate Church of
  Holy Trinity *64-7*
Walesby, All Saints *163*

Norfolk
Binham, Binham Priory *116*
Ranworth, St Helen *137*
Sparham, St Mary the Virgin *140*
Walpole St Peter, St Peter *105-6*
West Walton, St Mary the Virgin *53*
Wiggenhall St Peter, St Peter *156*

Northamptonshire
Brixworth, All Saints *22*
Hexham, Hexham Abbey *57*

Nottinghamshire
Babworth, All Saints *115*
Fotheringhay, St Mary & All Saints *120*

Oxfordshire
Burford, St John the Baptist *119*
Ewelme, St Mary the Virgin *139*
Iffley, St Mary the Virgin *49*
Little Farringdon, St Margaret *54*

Somerset
Culbone, St Beuno *109*
Isle Abbotts, St Mary the Virgin *70*
Mells, St Andrew *124-6*

South Yorkshire
Fishlake, St Cuthbert *60*

Suffolk
Blythburgh, Holy Trinity *130*
Ufford, St Mary of the Assumption *133*
Wenhaston, St Peter *144*
Woolpit, St Mary the Virgin *73*

Surrey
Chaldon, St Peter & St Paul *143*
Compton, Watts Cemetery Chapel *98*

Wiltshire
Bradford-on-Avon, St Laurence *33*
Inglesham, St John the Baptist *109-10*
Lacock, St Cyriac *168*
Old Dilton, St Mary *79*
Steeple Ashton, Priory Church of
  St Mary the Virgin *67-8*

Worcestershire
Croome D'Abitot, St Mary Magdalene *76*

About the illustrator

Ioana Pioaru is a Romanian-British artist living in West Sussex, UK. She works with a variety of media, ranging from traditional drawing and printmaking to VR art-making and holography. She has developed an extensive exhibition record which includes national and international solo and group shows. Ioana received her BA (2008) and MA (2010) from the National University of Arts in Bucharest, where she studied fine art drawing. In 2021 she was awarded a doctoral degree by the University of Chester for her research into the concept of artistic maximalism.

Quarto

First published in 2025 by Frances Lincoln, an imprint of The Quarto Group. One Triptych Place, London SE1 9SH, United Kingdom (0)20 7700 9000 www.Quarto.com

EEA Representation, WTS Tax d.o.o., Žanova ulica 3, 4000 Kranj, Slovenia

Text © 2025 Luke Sherlock
Illustrations © 2025 Ioana Pioaru
Design Copyright © 2025 Quarto Publishing plc

Printed in China

A catalogue record for this book is available from the British Library.

ISBN 978-0-7112-9410-3

e-Book ISBN 978-0-7112-9411-0

10 9 8 7 6 5 4 3

Commissioning Editor John Parton
Editor Aruna Vasudevan
Designer Myfanwy Vernon-Hunt
Senior Editor Michael Brunström
Senior Designer Isabel Eeles
Production Controller Alex Merrett

MIX
Paper | Supporting responsible forestry
FSC
www.fsc.org
FSC® C016973